MONEY MAGIC!

MONEY MAGIC

WALLACE D. WATTLES
The Science of Getting Rich

———◆———

JOSEPH MURPHY
How to Attract Money

———◆———

CLAUDE M. BRISTOL
The Magic of Believing

ABRIDGED AND INTRODUCED BY
MITCH HOROWITZ

Published by Gildan Media LLC
aka G&D Media.
www.GandDmedia.com

The Science of Getting Rich was originally published in 1910
How to Attract Money was originally published in 1955
The Magic of Believing was originally published in 1948
G&D Media Condensed Classics edition published 2018
Abridgement and Introduction copyright © 2018 by Mitch
Horowitz

FIRST EDITION: 2018

Cover design by David Rheinhardt of Pyrographx

Interior design by Meghan Day Healey of Story Horse, LLC.

ISBN: 978-1-7225-0092-4

Contents

Introduction

Is Money Magic a Real Thing?
By Mitch Horowitz

C an a book bring you riches—or, at least, cold hard cash? I wouldn't be too quick to answer that question until you personally experiment with the condensed works in this collection.

I have written many times that we live under multiple laws and forces. There are myriad factors behind the ebb and flow of money in our lives. But I firmly believe that our thoughts about money are among them. For that reason, the discovery of a new set of ideas and beliefs about money can, potentially, have a radical effect.

That is exactly what you will discover in the three abridged works in this collection: *The Science of Getting Rich; How to Attract Money*; and *The Magic of Believing*. More so, these books get you asking about—and experimenting with—how your thoughts relate to and impact your personal resources.

I want to share a very unusual—and entirely true— story about one of the books in this collection, Claude

M. Bristol's *The Magic of Believing*. This book, which you may have never before encountered, has played a vital role in the lives of people you have likely heard of. Pianist Liberace, comedienne Phyllis Diller, and radio host George Noory have sworn by Bristol's volume as the source of their success. This leads to my story.

I have a close friend in New England who had been recovering from a serious illness. Several months before this writing, he hit financial bottom. He had a total of $102 to his name. Despite his various efforts, he had lost his health insurance and was facing financial catastrophe.

One February night in 2018, he encountered my challenge on social media to make a fresh reading of Bristol's 1948 classic. Feeling he had little left to lose, my friend went on a marathon listening spree of an audio edition that I happened to narrate. He listened to it through for several days.

He called me breathlessly one morning. A boss from an old job phoned him to say that he needed to do something about his dormant 401k. "Oh that?" he asked indifferently, thinking it was just a few dollars and cents. "Have you looked at it lately?" his ex-boss asked. The all-but-forgotten account held $52,000.

The news arrived, literally, like a miracle. I define a miracle, quite simply, as a fortuitous departure from all reasonable expectation. As life visits frictions and tragedies on us, it also visits fantastically unexpected good news. An actuary can crunch the numbers, and I'm not necessarily asserting a "magical" cause and effect. But the timing and emotions left my friend with an indelible sense of meaning.

Many vintage mind-power books, like the ones in this collection, tantalize readers with stories of miraculous outcomes. (The disappointments are notably absent.) "Where are *today's* miracles?" I get asked.

Well, I've just given you one to judge. More importantly, I ask you to read and apply the ideas in this volume—do so fully, with passion, and without reservation. See what happens. And then answer for yourself the question I opened with.

THE SCIENCE OF
GETTING RICH

THE SCIENCE OF GETTING RICH

by Wallace D. Wattles

*The Legendary Mental Program
to Wealth and Mastery*

Abridged and Introduced
by Mitch Horowitz

THE CONDENSED CLASSICS LIBRARY™

Contents

The Ethic of Success

Some people have deeply contradictory feelings about the idea of "getting rich." They believe that getting rich sounds gauche, unspiritual, or selfish. This book by American social reformer and New Thought pioneer Wallace D. Wattles will put those mixed feelings to rest.

Wattles, a fighter for progressive causes as well as a pioneering mind theorist, believed that the true aim of enrichment was not the mere accumulation of personal resources, but the establishment of a better world: a world of shared abundance and possibility for all people.

His guidebook *The Science of Getting Rich* was obscure until about ten years ago. In 2007, word spread that *The Science of Getting Rich* was a source behind the mega-selling book and movie *The Secret*. The book began to hit bestseller lists, nearly than a century after

the author's death in 1911. I published an edition myself that reached number-one on the *Businessweek* bestseller list.

But what many of Wattles's new generation of readers missed was his dedication to the ethic of collective
advancement and creativity above animal competition;
his belief that competition itself was an outmoded idea,
soon to be supplanted but the creative capacities found
within the mind. And that once unlocked, these higher
capacities would grant working men and women the
keys to a life of prosperity for themselves and for all
around them.

Was his vision really so utopian? We live in an age
of remarkable advances in placebo studies, extending
even to "placebo surgery" and mentally based weight-
loss; new findings in the field called neuroplasticity,
which show that the brain's neural pathways are literally
"rewired" by habits of thought; extraordinary questions
posed by quantum physics experiments, which suggest
causality between thought and object; and ongoing and
serious experiments in ESP, which repeatedly demonstrate some kind of nonphysical conveyance of data in
laboratory settings.

Wattles's vision, now more than a century old, was
simply to ask whether these remarkable abilities, which
were only hinted at in the science labs of his day, could

be applied and experimented with on the material scale of daily life.

Wattles did not live long enough to see the influence of his book. He died of tuberculosis less than a year after it appeared. But his calm certainty and profoundly confident yet gentle tone suggest that he understood the portent of what he was writing.

Like every great thinker, Wattles left us not with a doctrine, but rather with articles of experimentation. The finest thing you can do to honor the memory of this good man—and to advance your own place in life—is to heed his advice: Go and experiment. Go and try. And if you experience results, as I think you will, do what he did: Tell the people.

—Mitch Horowitz

CHAPTER ONE

For Those Who Want Money

This book is a practical manual, not a treatise upon theories. It is intended for men and women whose most pressing need is money; who wish to get rich first, and philosophize afterward. It is for those who have, so far, found neither the time, the means, nor the opportunity to go deeply into the study of metaphysics, but who want results and who are willing to take the conclusions of science as a basis for action, without going into all the processes by which those conclusions were reached.

It is expected that the reader will take the fundamental statements of this book upon faith; and, taking the statements upon faith, that he will prove their truth by acting upon them without fear or hesitation.

Every man or woman who does this will certainly get rich; for the science herein is an exact science, and failure is impossible. For the benefit, however, of those who wish to investigate philosophical theories and secure a logical basis for faith, I will here cite certain authorities.

The monistic theory of the universe—the theory that One is All, and that All is One; that one Substance manifests itself as the seeming many elements of the material world—is of Hindu origin, and has been gradually winning its way into the thought of the western world for two hundred years. It is the foundation of all the Oriental philosophies, and of those of Descartes, Spinoza, Leibnitz, Schopenhauer, Hegel, and Emerson.

In writing this book I have sacrificed all other considerations to plainness and simplicity of style, so that all might understand. The plan of action laid down herein was deduced from the conclusions of philosophy; it has been thoroughly tested, and bears the supreme test of practical experiment: *it works*. If you wish to know how the conclusions were arrived at, read the writings of the authors mentioned above; and if you wish to reap the fruits of their philosophies in actual practice, read this book, and do exactly as it tells you to do.

Chapter Two

The Right to be Rich

The object of life is development; and everything that lives has an inalienable right to all the development that it is capable of attaining.

Man's right to life means his right to have the free and unrestricted use of all things necessary to his fullest mental, spiritual, and physical unfoldment; or, in other words, his right to be rich.

In this book, I do not speak of riches in a figurative way; to be really rich does not mean to be satisfied or contented with a little. No man ought to be satisfied with a little if he is capable of using and enjoying more. The purpose of Nature is the advancement and unfoldment of life; and every man should have all that can contribute to the power, elegance, beauty, and richness of life. To be content with less is sinful.

The desire for riches is really the desire for a richer, fuller, and more abundant life.

There are three motives for which we live: the body, the mind, and the soul. No one of these is better or holier than the other; all are alike desirable, and no one of the three—body, mind, or soul—can live fully if either of the others is cut short of full life and expression.

Real life means the complete expression of all that man can give forth through body, mind, and soul.

Wherever there is unexpressed possibility, or function not performed, there is unsatisfied desire. Desire is possibility seeking expression, or function seeking performance.

It is perfectly right that you should desire to be rich; if you are a normal man or woman you cannot help doing so. It is perfectly right that you should give your best attention to the Science of Getting Rich, for it is the noblest and most necessary of all studies. If you neglect this study, you are derelict in your duty to yourself, to God and humanity; for you can render to God and humanity no greater service than to make the most of yourself.

CHAPTER THREE

There Is a Science of Getting Rich

There is a Science of Getting Rich, and it is an exact science, like algebra or arithmetic. There are certain laws that govern the process of acquiring riches.

The ownership of money and property comes as a result of doing things in a *certain way*; those who do things in this Certain Way, whether on purpose or accidentally, get rich; while those who do not do things in this Certain Way, no matter how hard they work or how able they are, remain poor.

The ability to do things in this certain way is not due solely to birth or talent, for many people who have great talent remain poor, while others who have little talent get rich.

Studying the people who have gotten rich, we find that they are an average lot in all respects, having no greater talents and abilities than other men. It is evident that they do not get rich because they possess talents and abilities that other men have not, but because they happen to do things in a Certain Way.

Some degree of ability to think and understand is, of course, essential; but insofar as natural ability is concerned, any man or woman who has sense enough to read and understand these words can get rich.

It is true that you will do best in a business that you like, and that is congenial to you; and if you have certain talents that are well developed, you will do best in a business that calls for those talents.

Also, you will do best in a business that is suited to your locality; an ice-cream parlor would do better in a warm climate than in Greenland, and a salmon fishery will succeed better in the Northwest than in Florida, where there are no salmon.

But, aside from these general limitations, getting rich is not dependent upon your engaging in some particular business, but upon your learning to do things in a Certain Way that causes success. It is this to which we now turn.

CHAPTER FOUR

Is Opportunity Monopolized?

I t is quite true that if you are a workman in the employ of the steel trust you have very little chance of becoming the owner of the plant for which you work; but it is also true that if you will commence to act in a Certain Way, you can soon leave the employ of the steel trust for new opportunity.

At different periods the tide of opportunity sets in different directions, according to the needs of the whole, and the particular stage of social evolution that has been reached.

There is abundance of opportunity for the man who will go with the tide, instead of trying to swim against it.

The workers are not being "kept down" by their masters. As a class, they are where they are because they do not do things in a Certain Way. If the workers of America chose to do so, they could follow the example of their brothers in Belgium and other countries, and establish great department stores and co-operative industries; they could elect men of their own class to office, and pass laws favoring the development of such co-operative industries; and in a few years they could take peaceable possession of the industrial field.

The working class may become the master class whenever they will begin to do things in a Certain Way; the law of wealth is the same for them as it is for all others. This they must learn; and they will remain where they are as long as they continue to do as they do. The individual worker, however, is not held down by the ignorance or the mental slothfulness of his class; he can follow the tide of opportunity to riches.

The visible supply is practically inexhaustible; and the invisible supply really IS inexhaustible.

Everything you see on earth is made from one original substance, out of which all things proceed.

New forms are constantly being made, and older ones are dissolving; but all are shapes assumed by One Thing.

There is no limit to the supply of Formless Stuff, or Original Substance. The universe is made out of it; but it was not all used in making the universe. The spaces in, through, and between the forms of the visible universe are permeated and filled with the Original Substance; with the formless Stuff; with the raw material of all things. Ten thousand times as much as has been made might still be made, and even then we should not have exhausted the supply of universal raw material.

Nature is an inexhaustible storehouse of riches; the supply will never run short. Original Substance is alive with creative energy, and is constantly producing more forms. When the supply of building material is exhausted, more will be produced; when the soil is exhausted so that foodstuffs and materials for clothing will no longer grow upon it, it will be renewed or more soil will be made. When all the gold and silver has been dug from the earth, if man is still in such a stage of social development that he needs gold and silver, more will produced from the Formless. The Formless Stuff responds to the needs of man; it will not let him be without any good thing.

The Formless Stuff is intelligent; it is stuff that thinks. It is alive, and is always impelled toward more life.

It is the natural and inherent impulse of life to seek to live more; it is the nature of intelligence to enlarge itself, and of consciousness to seek to extend its boundaries and find fuller expression. The universe of forms has been made by Formless Living Substance, throwing itself into form in order to express itself more fully.

The universe is a great Living Presence, always moving inherently toward more life and fuller functioning.

Nature is formed for the advancement of life; its impelling motive is the increase of life. For this cause, everything that can possibly minister to life is bountifully provided; there can be no lack unless God is to contradict himself and nullify his own works.

I shall demonstrate shortly that the resources of the Formless Supply are at the command of the man or woman who will act and think in a Certain Way.

CHAPTER FIVE

The First Principle in the Science of Getting Rich

T hought is the only power that can produce tangible riches from the Formless Substance. The stuff from which all things are made is a substance that thinks, and a thought of form in this substance produces the form.

Original Substance moves according to its thoughts; every form and process you see in nature is the visible expression of a thought in Original Substance. As the Formless Stuff thinks of a form, it takes that form; as it thinks of a motion, it makes that motion. That is the way all things were created. We live in a thought world, which is part of a thought universe. The thought of a moving universe extended throughout Formless Substance, and the Thinking Stuff moving according to that thought, took the form of systems of planets, and maintains that form. Thinking Substance takes the form of its thought, and moves according to the thought.

Every thought of form held in thinking Substance, causes the creation of the form but always, or at least generally, along lines of growth and action already established.

No thought of form can be impressed upon Original Substance without causing the creation of the form.

Man is a thinking center, and can originate thought. All the forms that man fashions with his hands must first exist in his thought; he cannot shape a thing until he has thought that thing.

Yet so far man has confined his efforts wholly to the work of his hands; he has applied manual labor to the world of forms, seeking to change or modify what already exists. He has never thought of trying to cause the creation of new forms by impressing his thoughts upon Formless Substance.

As our first step, we must lay down three fundamental propositions:

1) There is a thinking stuff from which all things are made, and which, in its original state, permeates, penetrates, and fills the interspaces of the universe.

2) A thought, in this substance, produces the thing that is imaged by the thought.

3) Man can form things in his thought, and, by impressing his thought upon formless substance, can cause the thing he thinks about to be created.

Read these creed statements over and over again; fix every word upon your memory, and meditate upon them until you firmly believe what they say.

There is no labor from which most people shrink as they do from that of sustained and consecutive thought; it is the hardest work in the world. This is especially true when truth is contrary to appearances. Every appearance in the visible world tends to produce a corresponding form in the mind that observes it; and this can be prevented only by holding the thought of the TRUTH.

Do not ask why these things are true, nor speculate as to how they can be true; simply take them on trust.

The science of getting rich begins with the absolute acceptance of this faith.

CHAPTER SIX

Increasing Life

The desire for riches is simply the capacity for larger life seeking fulfillment; every desire is the effort of an unexpressed possibility to come into action. It is power seeking to manifest that causes desire. That which makes you want more money is the same as that which makes the plant grow: it is Life, seeking fuller expression.

The One Living Substance must be subject to this inherent law of all life; it is permeated with the desire to live more; that is why it is under the necessity of creating things.

It is the desire of God that you should get rich. He wants you to get rich because He can express himself better through you if you have plenty of things to use in giving Him expression. He can live more in you if you have unlimited command of the means of life.

The universe desires you to have everything you want to have.

Nature is friendly to your plans.

Everything is naturally for you.

Make up your mind that this is true.

It is essential, however that *your purpose should harmonize with the purpose that is in All.*

You must want real life, not mere pleasure of sensual gratification. Life is the performance of function; and the individual really lives only when he performs every function, physical, mental, and spiritual, of which he is capable, without excess in any.

Remember, however, that the desire of Substance is for all, and its movements must be for more life to all; it cannot be made to work for less life to any, because it is equally in all, seeking riches and life.

Intelligent Substance will make things for you, but it will not take things away from some one else and give them to you.

You are to become a creator, not a competitor; you are going to get what you want, but in such a way that when you get it every other man will have more than he has now.

I am aware that there are men who get a vast amount of money by proceeding in direct opposition to the statements above, and may add a word of explanation here. Men of the plutocratic type, who become very rich, do so sometimes purely by their extraordinary ability on the plane of competition; and sometimes they unconsciously relate themselves to Substance in its great purposes and movements for the general racial upbuilding through industrial evolution. Rockefeller, Carnegie, Morgan, et al., have been the unconscious agents of the Supreme in the necessary work of systematizing and organizing productive industry; and in the end, their work will contribute immensely toward increased life for all. Their day is nearly over; they have organized production, and *will soon be succeeded by the agents of the multitude, who will organize the machinery of distribution.*

The multi-millionaires are like the monster reptiles of the prehistoric eras; they play a necessary part in the evolutionary process, but the same Power that produced them will dispose of them. And it is well to bear in mind that they have never been really rich; a record of the private lives of most of this class will show that they have really been the most abject and wretched of the poor.

Riches secured on the competitive plane are never satisfactory and permanent; they are yours today, and another's tomorrow. Remember, if you are to become rich in a scientific and certain way, you must rise entirely out of the competitive thought.

Let us consider once more:

There is a thinking stuff from which all things are made, and which, in its original state, permeates, penetrates, and fills the interspaces of the universe.

A thought, in this substance, produces the thing that is imaged by the thought.

Man can form things in his thought, and, by impressing his thought upon formless substance, can cause the thing he thinks about to be created.

The supply is limitless.

Chapter Seven

How Riches Come to You

When I say that you do not have to drive sharp bargains, I do not mean that you do not have to drive any bargains at all, or that you are above the necessity for having any dealings with your fellow men. I mean that you will not need to deal with them unfairly; you do not have to get something for nothing, *but can give to every man more than you take from him.*

You cannot give every man more in cash market value than you take from him, but you can give him more in use value than the cash value of the thing you take from him. The paper, ink, and other material in this book may not be worth the money you pay for it; but if the ideas suggested by it bring you thousands of dollars, you have not been wronged by those who sold it to you; they have given you a great use value for a small cash value.

Give every man more in use value than you take from him in cash value; then you are adding to the life of the world by every business transaction.

If you have people working for you, you must take from them more in cash value than you pay them in wages; but you can so organize your business that it will be filled with the principle of advancement, and so that each employee who wishes to do so may advance a little every day.

You can make your business do for your employees what this book is doing for you. You can so conduct your business that it will be a sort of ladder, by which every employee who will take the trouble may climb to riches himself; and given the opportunity, if he will not do so it is not your fault.

Chapter Eight

Gratitude

The whole process of mental adjustment and atonement can be summed up in one word: gratitude.

First, you believe that there is one Intelligent Substance, from which all things proceed; second, you believe that this Substance gives you everything you desire; and third, you relate yourself to it by a feeling of deep and profound gratitude.

Many people who order their lives rightly in all other ways are kept in poverty by their lack of gratitude. Having received one gift from God, they cut the wires that connect them with Him by failing to make acknowledgment.

It is easy to understand that the nearer we live to the source of wealth, the more wealth we shall receive; and it is easy also to understand that the soul that is always grateful lives in closer touch with God than the one that never looks to Him in thankful acknowledgment.

The more gratefully we fix our minds on the Supreme when good things come to us, the more good things we will receive, and the more rapidly they will come; and the reason simply is that the mental attitude of gratitude draws the mind into closer touch with the source from which the blessings come.

There is a Law of Gratitude, and it is absolutely necessary that you should observe the law, if you are to get the results you seek.

The Law of Gratitude is the natural principle that action and reaction are always equal, and in opposite directions.

The grateful outreaching of your mind in thankful praise to the Supreme *is a liberation or expenditure of force; it cannot fail to reach that to which it addressed, and the reaction is an instantaneous movement towards you.*

"Draw nigh unto God, and He will draw nigh unto you." That is a statement of psychological truth.

Chapter Nine

Thinking in a Certain Way

I t is not enough that you should have a general desire for wealth "to do good." Everybody has that desire.

It is not enough that you should have a wish to travel, see things, live more, etc. Everybody has those desires, too. If you were going to relay a radio message to a friend, you would not send the letters of the alphabet in their order, and let him construct the message for himself; nor would you take words at random from the dictionary. You would send a coherent sentence; one that meant something.

When you try to impress your wants upon Substance it must be done by a coherent statement; you must know what you want, and be definite. You can never get rich, or start the creative power into action, by sending out unformed longings and vague desires.

You must have a clear mental picture continually in mind, and you must keep your face toward it all the time.

It is not necessary to take exercises in concentration, nor to set apart special times for prayer and affirmation. These things are well enough, but all you need is to know what you want, and to want it badly enough so that it will stay in your thoughts.

Spend as much of your leisure time as you can in contemplating your picture, but no one needs to take exercises to concentrate his mind on a thing that he really wants; it is the things you do not really care about that require effort to focus upon.

The more clear and definite you make your picture then, and the more you dwell upon it, bringing out all its delightful details, the stronger your desire will be; and the stronger your desire, the easier it will be to hold your mind fixed upon the picture of what you want.

Something more is necessary, however, than merely to see the picture clearly.

Behind your clear vision must be the purpose to realize it; to bring it out in tangible expression.

And behind this purpose must be an invincible and unwavering FAITH that the thing is already yours; that it is "at hand" and you have only to take possession of it.

Live in the new house, mentally, until it takes form around you physically. In the mental realm, enter at once into full enjoyment of the things you want.

"Whatsoever things ye ask for when ye pray, believe that ye receive them, and ye shall have them," said Jesus.

You do not need to pray repeatedly for things you want; it is not necessary to tell God about it every day.

"Use not vain repetitions as the heathen do," Jesus told his pupils, "for your Father knoweth that ye have need of these things before ye ask Him."

Your part is to intelligently formulate your desires for the things which make for a larger life, and to get these desires arranged into a coherent whole; and then to impress this Whole Desire upon the Formless Substance, which has the power and the will to bring you what you want.

You do not make this impression by repeating strings of words; you make it by holding the vision with unshakable PURPOSE to attain it, and with steadfast FAITH that you do attain it.

The answer to prayer is not according to your faith while you are talking, but according to your faith while you are working.

CHAPTER TEN

How to Use the Will

To set about getting rich in a scientific way, do not try to apply your will power to anything outside of yourself.

You have no right to, anyway.

It is wrong to apply your will to other men and women in order to get them to do what you wish done.

It is as flagrantly wrong to coerce people by mental power as it is to coerce them by physical power. If compelling people by physical force to do things for you reduces them to slavery, compelling them by mental means accomplishes the same thing.

You have no right to use your will power upon another person, even "for his own good;" for you do not know what is for his good.

To get rich, you need only to use your will power upon yourself.

When you know what to think and do, then you must use your will to compel yourself to think and do the right things. That is the legitimate use of the will in getting what you want—to use it in holding yourself to the right course. Use your will to keep yourself thinking and acting in the Certain Way.

Do not try to project your will, or your thoughts, or your mind out into space, to "act" on things or people.

Keep your mind at home; it can accomplish more there than elsewhere.

Use your mind to form a mental image of what you want, and to hold that vision with faith and purpose; and use your will to keep your mind working in the Right Way.

The more steady and continuous your faith and purpose, the more rapidly you will get rich, because you will make only POSITIVE impressions upon Substance; and you will not neutralize or offset them by negative impressions.

The picture of your desires, held with faith and purpose, is taken up by the Formless. As this impression spreads, all things are set moving toward its realization; every living thing, every inanimate thing, and the things yet uncreated, are stirred toward bringing into being that which you want. All force begins to be exerted in that direction; all things begin to move toward you. The minds of people, everywhere, are influenced toward doing the things necessary to the fulfilling of your desires; and they work for you, unconsciously.

Since belief is all-important, it behooves you to guard your thoughts; and as your beliefs will be shaped to a very great extent by the things you observe and think about, it is important that you should command your attention.

Chapter Eleven

Further Use of the Will

Y ou cannot retain a true and clear vision of wealth if you are constantly turning your attention to opposing pictures, whether they are external or imaginary.

Do not tell of your past troubles of a financial nature; if you have had them, do not think of them at all. Do not tell of the poverty of your parents, or the hardships of your early life; to do any of these things is to mentally class yourself with the poor for the time being, and it will certainly check the movement of things in your direction.

"Let the dead bury their dead," as Jesus said.

Put poverty and all things that pertain to poverty completely behind you.

You have accepted a certain theory of the universe as being correct, and are resting all your hopes of happiness on its being correct; and what can you gain by giving heed to conflicting theories?

You can aim at nothing so great or noble, I repeat, as to become rich; and you must fix your attention upon your mental picture of riches, to the exclusion of all that may tend to dim or obscure the vision.

You must learn to see the underlying TRUTH in all things; you must see beneath all seemingly wrong conditions the Great One Life ever moving forward toward fuller expression and more complete happiness.

The very best thing you can do for the whole world is to make the most of yourself.

Chapter Twelve

Acting in the Certain Way

This is the crucial point in the Science of Getting Rich—right here, where thought and personal action must be combined. Many people, consciously or unconsciously, set the creative forces in action by the strength and persistence of their desires, yet they remain poor because they do not provide for the reception of the thing they want when it comes.

By thought, the thing you want is brought to you; by action you receive it.

Whatever your action is to be, it is evident that you must act NOW. You cannot act in the past, and it is essential to the clearness of your mental vision that you dismiss the past from your mind. You cannot act in the future, for the future is not here yet. And you cannot tell how you will want to act in any future contingency until that contingency has arrived.

Because you are not in the right business, or the right environment now, do not think that you must postpone action until you get into the right business or environment. And do not spend time in the present taking thought as to the best course in possible future emergencies; have faith in your ability to meet any emergency when it arrives.

Put your whole mind into present action.

Do not bother as to whether yesterday's work was well done or ill done; do to-day's work well.

Do not try to do tomorrow's work now; there will be plenty of time to do that when you get to it.

Do not try, by occult or mystical means, to act on people or things that are out of your reach.

Do not wait for a change of environment, before you act; get a change of environment by action.

You can so act upon the environment in which you are now, as to cause yourself to be transferred to a better environment.

Hold with faith and purpose the vision of yourself in the better environment, but act upon your present environment with all your heart, and with all your strength, and with all your mind.

You can advance only by being larger than your present place; and no man is larger than his present place who leaves undone any of the work pertaining to that place.

Doing what you want to do is life; and there is no real satisfaction in living if we are compelled to be forever doing something that we do not like to do. And it is certain that you can do what you want because the *desire* to do it is proof that you have within you the power that *can* do it.

Desire is a manifestation of power.

The desire to play music is the power that can play music seeking expression and development.

If there are past mistakes whose consequences have placed you in an undesirable business or environment, you may be obliged for some time to do that which you do not like to do; but you can make the doing of it pleasant by knowing that it is making it possible for you to come to the doing of what you want to do.

Remember always that definiteness of purpose, the ability of your thoughts to impress themselves upon the great Original Substance of the universe, the sincere impulse toward creative function, the desire to build—not to best—your neighbor, and the dedication to doing all you can wherever you are, place at your back an awesome power of Truth, to which nothing can be denied.

Build the world that you dream of for yourself and others; bring prosperity and beauty into creation; improve yourself—and you improve the world. That is the noblest goal to which any man or woman can aspire.

About the Authors

A progressive social reformer and New Thought pioneer, WALLACE D. WATTLES was born in 1860 in the United States. He popularized creative-thought principles in his groundbreaking classics *The Science of Getting Rich*, *The Science of Being Great*, and *The Science of Being Well*. A great influence on future generations of success writers, he died in 1911.

MITCH HOROWITZ, who abridged and introduced this volume, is the PEN Award-winning author of books including *Occult America* and *The Miracle Club: How Thoughts Become Reality*. *The Washington Post* says Mitch "treats esoteric ideas and movements with an even-handed intellectual studiousness that is too often lost in today's raised-voice discussions." Follow him @MitchHorowitz.

How to
Attract
Money

HOW TO
ATTRACT
MONEY

by Joseph Murphy

The Original Classic of Abundance—
from the Author of
The Power of Your Subconscious Mind

Abridged and Introduced
by Mitch Horowitz

THE CONDENSED CLASSICS LIBRARY™

Contents

The Book You've Been Waiting For

I am often asked: If I were to select one New Thought book to recommend to someone approaching the philosophy of mental causation for the first time, or maybe someone who is willing to sample one and just one book, which would it be?

The answer has eluded me. I have been uncertain whether to recommend a "mainstream" work like Earl Nightingale's wonderful lecture *The Strangest Secret*, which lays out New Thought in a precise, businesslike manner, omitting most mystical themes. For someone from a strictly nonreligious background, I might recommend surgeon Maxwell Maltz's *Psycho-Cybernetics*, which is a secular, psychological exploration of the mind's formative abilities. Or, finally, if I see that someone has a key goal in mind, and is open to both spiritual and psychological language, I would recommend Napoleon Hill's evergreen *Think and Grow Rich*.

But in writing these words, I realize that the book I should be recommending—and that I plan to from now on—is one that I've been reading for years, but never fully appreciated: Joseph Murphy's slender 1955 masterpiece, *How to Attract Money*.

I think that I have previously resisted recommending *How to Attract Money* because I felt slightly embarrassed by its acquisitive-sounding title. Thoughtful people are taught to believe that overt expressions of money-getting are vulgar or "unspiritual." Reading this book with fresh eyes, however, I am disabused of that notion. First of all, money—in whatever form it takes, whether bills, goods, or commodities—is part of the natural human exchange, and is indelibly tied to all phases of our lives. More importantly, Murphy, in his genius as a communicator, uses the topic of money, something that we all need, as a metaphor for the point he's really making: which is that we are generative, causative beings who channel the power of higher creativity through the medium of our thoughts, which take form in the overt circumstances of our lives.

Not everyone approaching New Thought, or this book, must be spiritual in outlook. One could venture psychological explanations for the link between

thoughts and events, something that Maltz does com-
pellingly in *Psycho-Cybernetics*, where he compares the
mind to a homing device, like a heat-seeking missile,
which is programed by our subconscious beliefs. And
that is valid. But New Thought, at its heart, is spiritual,
by which I mean it posits a non-material, extra-physical
basis for life. In this short volume, Joseph Murphy explains this perspective, and provides precise techniques
for using your thoughts, prayers, mental images, and
affirmations in a manner that exerts and channels the
creative intelligence of cosmos, or what we call God.

When Murphy writes about using the powers of
your mind while in a drowsy, pre-sleep state, and when
he asserts that the Bible is a symbolical book of inner
development, his ideas converge with those of his con-
temporary seeker, spiritual teacher Neville Goddard.
Murphy recalled studying with Neville (who wrote
under his first name) when the two men—Murphy a
recent immigrant from Ireland and Neville from the
West Indies—were coming up as metaphysical teach-
ers on the New York scene in the 1930s. In interviews
toward the end of his life in 1981, Murphy said that
he and Neville shared the same teacher: a mysterious,
turbaned black rabbi named Abdullah.

If all that is a little too mystical for you, don't worry.
Murphy's philosophy doesn't require credulity; it requires

experimentation. And the experiments in this book are exquisitely private—they are yours alone. They require no membership or label. And, most especially, there is no need to disclose what you're doing to anyone else. In fact, it's better not to. These ideas don't need another's approval or approbation—only your engagement.

This short book, written eight years before the 1963 publication of Murphy's worldwide bestseller *The Power of Your Subconscious Mind*, captured his philosophy in its totality. Murphy's communicative powers, always considerable, are at their peak. His words here are effective, truthful, and, I think, demonstrably good and beneficent.

I have been reading New Thought literature for about twenty years, and yet *something*—I cannot quite say what—awakened in me when I recently reread this little book in the early morning hours, while my home in New York City remained covered in predawn darkness and the activity of the streets was briefly stilled. I wish a similar experience for you. And if you, like me, come to feel that you want to share this book with friends and curious people, you will be spreading seeds of mental creativity, which may grow in your life and in the lives of others in ways that surprise you. That, too, I wish for all who approach this volume.

—Mitch Horowitz
New York City, 2017

CHAPTER ONE

Your Right to be Rich

I t is your right to be rich. You are here to lead the abundant life, and be happy, radiant, and free. You should, therefore, have all the money you need to lead a full, happy, prosperous life.

There is no virtue in poverty; the latter is a mental disease, and it should be abolished from the face of the earth. You are here to grow, expand, and unfold, spiritually, mentally, and materially. You have the inalienable right to fully develop and express yourself along all lines. You should surround yourself with beauty and luxury.

Why be satisfied with just enough to go around when you can enjoy the riches of the Infinite? In this book you will learn to make friends with money, and you will always have a surplus. Your desire to be rich is a desire for a fuller, happier, more wonderful life. It is a cosmic urge. It is good and very good.

Begin to see money in its true significance—as a symbol of exchange. It means to you freedom from want, and beauty, luxury, abundance, and refinement.

As you read this chapter, you are probably saying, "I want more money." "I am worthy of a higher salary than I am receiving."

I believe most people are inadequately compensated. One of the causes many people do not have more money is that they are silently or openly condemning it. They refer to money as "filthy lucre," or "Love of money is the root of all evil," etc. Another reason they do not prosper is that they have a sneaky, subconscious feeling there is some virtue in poverty; this subconscious pattern may be due to early childhood training, superstition, or it could be based on a false interpretation of the Scriptures.

There is no virtue in poverty; it is a disease like any other mental disease. If you were physically ill, you would think there was something wrong with you; you would seek help, or do something about the condition at once. Likewise if you do not have money constantly circulating in your life, there is something radically wrong with you.

Money is only a symbol; it has taken many forms as a medium of exchange down through the centuries, such as salt, beads, and trinkets of various kinds. In early times man's wealth was determined by the number of sheep or oxen he had. It is much more convenient to write a check than to carry some sheep around with you to pay your bills.

God does not want you to live in a hovel or go hungry. God wants you to be happy, prosperous, and successful. God is always successful in all His undertakings, whether He makes a star or a cosmos!

You may wish to make a trip around the world, study art in foreign countries, go to college, or send your children to a superior school. You certainly wish to bring your children up in lovely surroundings, so that they might learn to appreciate beauty, order, symmetry, and proportion.

You were born to succeed, to win, to conquer all difficulties, and have all your faculties fully developed. If there is financial lack in your life, do something about it.

Get away immediately from all superstitious beliefs about money. Do not ever regard money as evil or filthy. If you do, you cause it to take wings and fly away from you. Remember that you lose what you condemn.

Suppose, for example, you found gold, silver, lead, copper, or iron in the ground. Would you pronounce these things evil? God pronounced all things good. The evil comes from man's darkened understanding, from his unillumined mind, from his false interpretation of life, and his misuse of Divine Power. Uranium, lead, or some other metal could have been used as a medium of exchange. We use paper bills, checks, etc.; surely the piece of paper is not evil; neither is the check. Physicists and scientists know today that the only difference between one metal and another is the number and rate of motion of the electrons revolving around a central nucleus. They are now changing one metal into another through a bombardment of the atoms in the powerful cyclotron. Gold under certain conditions becomes mercury. It will only be a little while until gold, silver, and other metals will be made synthetically in the chemical laboratory. I cannot imagine seeing anything evil in electrons, neutrons, protons, and isotopes.

The piece of paper in your pocket is composed of electrons and protons arranged differently; their number and rate of motion is different; that is the only way the paper differs from the silver in your pocket.

Some people will say, "Oh, people kill for money. They steal for money!" It has been associated with countless crimes, but that does not make it evil.

A man may give another $50 to kill someone; he has misused money in using it for a destructive purpose. You can use electricity to kill someone or light the house. You can use water to quench the baby's thirst, or use it to drown the child. You can use fire to warm the child, or burn it to death.

Another illustration would be if you brought some earth from your garden, put it in your coffee cup for breakfast, that would be your evil; yet the earth is not evil; neither is the coffee. The earth is displaced; it belongs in your garden.

Similarly if a needle were stuck in your thumb, it would be your evil; the needle or pin belongs in the pin cushion, not in your thumb.

We know the forces or the elements of nature are not evil; it depends on our use of them whether they bless or hurt us.

A man said to me one time, "I am broke. I do not like money; it is the root of all evil."

Love of money to the exclusion of everything else will cause you to become lopsided and unbalanced. You are here to use your power or authority wisely. Some men crave power; others crave money. If you set your heart on money, and say, "That is all I want. I am going to give all my attention to amassing money; nothing else matters," you can get money and attain a fortune, but you have forgotten that you are here to lead a balanced life. "Man does not live by bread alone."

For example, if you belong to some cult or religious group, and become fanatical about it, excluding yourself from your friends, society, and social activities, you will become unbalanced, inhibited, and frustrated. Nature insists on a balance. If all your time is devoted to external things and possessions, you will find yourself hungry for peace of mind, harmony, love, joy, or perfect health. You will find you cannot buy anything that is real. You can amass a fortune, or have millions of dollars; this is not evil or bad. Love of money to the exclusion of everything else results in frustration, disappointment, and disillusionment; in that sense it is the root of your evil.

By making money your sole aim, you simply made a wrong choice. You thought that was all you wanted, but you found after all your efforts that it was not only the money you needed. What you really desired was true place, peace of mind, and abundance. You could have the million or many millions, if you wanted them, and still have peace of mind, harmony, perfect health, and Divine Expression.

Everyone wants enough money, and not just enough to go around. He wants abundance and to spare; he should have it. The urges, desires, and impulses we have for food, clothing, homes, better means of transportation, expression, procreation, and abundance are all God-given, Divine, and good, but we may misdirect these impulses, desires, and urges resulting in evil or negative experiences in our lives.

Man does not have an evil nature; there is no evil nature in you; it is God, the Universal Wisdom, or Life seeking expression through you.

For example, a boy wants to go to college, but he does not have enough money. He sees other boys in the neighborhood going off to college and the university; his desire increases. He says to himself, "I want an education, too." Such a youth may steal and embezzle money for the purpose of going to college. The desire to go to college was basically and fundamentally good; he misdirected that desire or urge by violating the laws of society, the cosmic law of harmony, or the golden rule; then he finds himself in trouble.

However if this boy knew the laws of mind, and his unqualified capacity through the use of the Spiritual Power to go to college, he would be free and not in jail. Who put him in jail? He placed himself there. The policeman who locked him up in prison was an instrument of the man- made laws which he violated. He first imprisoned himself in his mind by stealing and hurting others. Fear and a guilt consciousness followed; this is the prison of the mind followed by the prison walls made of bricks and stones.

Money is a symbol of God's opulence, beauty, refinement, and abundance, and it should be used wisely, judiciously, and constructively to bless humanity in countless ways. It is merely a symbol of the economic health of the nation. When your blood is circulating freely, you are healthy. When money is circulating freely in your life, you are economically healthy. When people begin to hoard money, to put it away in tin boxes, and become charged with fear, there is economic illness.

The crash of 1929 was a psychological panic; it was fear seizing the minds of people everywhere. It was a sort of negative, hypnotic spell.

You are living in a subjective and objective world. You must not neglect the spiritual food, such as peace of mind, love, beauty, harmony, joy, and laughter.

Knowledge of the spiritual power is the means to the Royal Road to Riches of all kinds, whether your desire is spiritual, mental, or material. The student of the laws of mind, or the student of the spiritual principle, believes and knows absolutely that regardless of the economic situation, stock market fluctuation, depression, strikes, war, other conditions, or circumstances, he will always be amply supplied regardless of what form money may take. The reason for this is he abides in the consciousness of wealth. The student has convinced himself in his mind that wealth is forever flowing freely in his life, and that there is always a Divine surplus. Should there be a war tomorrow, and all the student's present holdings become valueless, as the

German marks did after the First World War, he would still attract wealth, and be cared for regardless of the form the new currency took.

Wealth is a state of consciousness; it is a mind conditioned to Divine supply forever flowing. The scientific thinker looks at money or wealth like the tide; i.e., it goes out, but it always comes back. The tides never fail; neither will man's supply when he trusts a tireless, changeless, immortal Presence which is Omnipresent, and flows ceaselessly. The man who knows the workings of the subconscious mind is never, therefore, worried about the economic situation, stock market panics, devaluation, or inflation of currency, since he abides in the consciousness of God's eternal supply. Such a man is always supplied and watched over by an overshadowing Presence. *Behold the fowls of the air: for they sow not, neither do they reap, nor gather into barns; yet your heavenly Father feedeth them. Are ye not much better than they?* MATTHEW 6:26

As you consciously commune with the Divine-Presence claiming and knowing that It leads and guides you in all your ways, that It is a Lamp unto your feet, and a Light on your path, you will be Divinely prospered and sustained beyond your wildest dreams.

Here is a simple way for you to impress your subconscious mind with the idea of constant supply or wealth: Quiet the wheels of your mind. Relax! Let go! Immobilize the attention. Get into a sleepy, drowsy, meditative state of mind; this reduces effort to the minimum; then in a quiet, relaxed, passive way reflect on the following simple truths: Ask yourself where do ideas come from? Where does wealth come from? Where did you come from? Where did your brain and your mind come from? You will be led back to the One Source.

You find yourself on a spiritual, working basis now. It will no longer insult your intelligence to realize that wealth is a state of mind. Take this little phrase; repeat it slowly four or five minutes three or four times a day quietly to yourself, particularly before you go to sleep: "Money is forever circulating freely in my life, and there is always a Divine surplus." As you do this regularly and systematically, the idea of wealth will be conveyed to your deeper mind, and you will develop a wealth consciousness. Idle, mechanical repetition will not succeed in building the consciousness of wealth. Begin to feel the truth of what you affirm. You know what you are doing, and why you are doing it. You know your deeper self is responsive to what you consciously accept as true.

In the beginning people who are in financial difficulties do not get results with such affirmations as, "I am wealthy," "I am prosperous," "I am successful"; such statements may cause their conditions to get worse. The reason is the subconscious mind will only accept the dominant of two ideas, or the dominant mood or feeling. When they say, "I am prosperous," their feeling of lack is greater, and something within them says, "No, you are not prosperous, you are broke." The feeling of lack is dominant so that each affirmation calls forth the mood of lack, and more lack becomes theirs. The way to overcome this for beginners is to affirm what the conscious and subconscious mind will agree on; then there will be no contradiction. Our subconscious mind accepts our beliefs, feelings, convictions, and what we consciously accept as true.

A man could engage the cooperation of his subconscious mind by saying, "I am prospering every day." "I am growing in wealth and in wisdom every day." "Every day my wealth is multiplying." "I am advancing, growing, and moving forward financially." These and similar statements would not create any conflict in the mind.

For instance if a salesman has only ten cents in his pocket, he could easily agree that he would have more tomorrow. If he sold a pair of shoes tomorrow, there is nothing within him which says his sales could not increase. He could use statements, such as, "My sales are increasing every day." "I am advancing and moving forward." He would find these would be sound psychologically, acceptable to his mind, and produce desirable fruit.

The spiritually advanced student who quietly, knowingly, and feelingly says, "I am prosperous," "I am successful," "I am wealthy," gets wonderful results also. Why would this be true? When they think, feel, or say, "I am prosperous," they mean God is All Supply or Infinite Riches, and what is true of God is true of them. When they say, "I am wealthy," they know God is Infinite Supply, the Inexhaustible, Treasure- House, and what is true of God is, therefore, true of them, for God is within them.

Many men get wonderful results by dwelling on three abstract ideas, such as health, wealth, and success. *Health* is a Divine Reality or quality of God. *Wealth* is of God; it is eternal and endless. *Success* is of God; God is always successful in all His undertakings.

The way they produce remarkable results is to stand before a mirror as they shave, and repeat for five or ten minutes: "Health, wealth, and success." They do not say, "I am healthy," or "I am successful"; they create no opposition in their minds. They are quiet and relaxed; thus the mind is receptive and passive; then they repeat these words. Amazing results follow. All they are doing is identifying with truths that are eternal, changeless, and timeless.

You can develop a wealth consciousness. Put the principles enunciated and elaborated on in this book to practice, and your desert will rejoice and blossom as the rose.

I worked with a young boy in Australia many years ago who wanted to become a physician and surgeon, but he had no money; nor had he graduated from high school. For expenses he used to clean out doctors' offices, wash windows, and do odd repair jobs. He told me that every night as he went to sleep, he used to see a diploma on a wall with his name in big, bold letters. He used to clean and shine the diplomas in the medical building where he worked; it was not hard for him to engrave the diploma in his mind and develop it there. I do not know how long he continued this imaging, but it must have been for some months.

Results followed as he persisted. One of the doctors took a great liking to this young boy, and after training him in the art of sterilizing instruments, giving hypodermic injections, and other miscellaneous first aid work, he became a technical assistant in his office. The doctor sent him to high school and also to college at his expense.

Today this man is a prominent doctor in Montreal, Canada. He had a dream! A clear image in his mind! *His wealth was in his mind.*

Wealth is your idea, desire, talent, urge for service, capacity to give to mankind, your ability for usefulness to society, and your love for humanity in general.

This young boy operated a great law unconsciously. Troward says, "Having seen the end, you have willed the means to the realization of the end." The end in this boy's case was to be a physician. To imagine, see, and feel the reality of being a doctor now, to live with that idea, sustain it, nourish it, and to love it until through his imagination it penetrated the layers of the subconscious, becoming a conviction, paved the way to the fulfillment of his dreams.

He could have said, "I have no education." "I do not know the right people." "I am too old to go to school now." "I have no money; it would take years, and I am not intelligent." He would then be beaten before he started. His wealth was in his use of the Spiritual Power within him which responded to his thought.

The means or the way in which our prayer is answered is always hidden from us except that occasionally we may intuitively perceive a part of the process. *My ways are past finding out.* The *ways* are not known. The only thing man has to do is to imagine and accept the end in his mind, and leave its unfoldment to the subjective wisdom within.

Oftentimes the question is asked, "What should I do after meditating on the end and accepting my desire in consciousness?" The answer is simple: You will be compelled to do whatever is necessary for the unfoldment of your ideal. The law of the subconscious is compulsion. The law of life is action and reaction. What we do is the automatic response to our inner movements of the mind, inner feeling, and conviction.

A few months ago as I went to sleep, I imagined I was reading one of my most popular books, *Magic of Faith* in French. I began to realize and imagine this book going into all French- speaking nations. For several weeks I did this every night, falling asleep with the imaginary French edition of *Magic of Faith* in my hands.

Just before Christmas in 1954, I received a letter from a leading publisher in Paris, France, enclosing a contract drawn up, asking me to sign it, giving him permission to publish and promote abroad to all French-speaking countries the French edition of *Magic of Faith*.

You might ask me what did I do about the publishing of this book after prayer? I would have to say, "Nothing!" The subjective wisdom took over, and brought it to pass in its own way, which was a far better way than any method I could consciously desire.

All of our external movements, motions, and actions follow the inner movements of the mind. Inner action precedes all outer action. Whatever steps you take physically, or what you seem to do objectively, will all be a part of a pattern which you were compelled to fulfill.

Accepting the end wills the means to the realization of the end. Believe that you have it now, and you shall receive it.

We must cease denying our good. Realize that the only thing that keeps us from the riches that lie all around us is our mental attitude, or the way we look at God, life, and the world in general. Know, believe, and act on the positive assumption that there is no reason why you cannot have, be, and do whatever you wish to accomplish through the great laws of God.

Your knowledge of how your mind works is your saviour and redeemer. Thought and feeling are your destiny. You possess everything by right of consciousness. The consciousness of health produces health; the consciousness of wealth produces wealth. The world seems to deny or oppose what you pray for; your senses sometimes mock and laugh at you.

If you say to your friend, you are opening up a new business for yourself, he may proceed to give you all the reasons why you are bound to fail. If you are susceptible to his hypnotic spell, he may instill fear of failure in your mind. As you become aware of the spiritual power which is one and indivisible, and responds to your thought, you will reject the darkness and ignorance of the world, and know that you possess all the equipment, power, and knowledge to succeed.

To walk on the Royal Road to Riches, you must not place obstacles and impediments on the pathway of others; neither must you be jealous or envious of others. Actually when you entertain these negative states of mind, you are hurting and injuring yourself, because you are thinking and feeling it. "The suggestion," as Quimby said, "you give to another, you are giving to yourself." This is the reason that the law of the golden rule is a cosmic, divine law.

I am sure you have heard men say, "That fellow has a racket." "He is a racketeer." "He is getting money dishonestly." "He is a faker." "I knew him when he had nothing." "He is crooked, a thief, and a swindler." If you analyze the man who talks like that, he is usually in want or suffering from some financial or physical illness. Perhaps his former, college friends went up the ladder of success and excelled him; now he is bitter and envious of their progress. In many instances this is the cause of his downfall. Thinking negatively of these classmates, and condemning their wealth, causes the wealth and prosperity he is praying for to vanish and flee away. He is condemning the things he is praying for. He is pray-ing two ways. On the one hand he is saying, "God is prospering me," and in the next breath, silently or audi-bly, he is saying, "I resent that fellow's wealth." Always make it a special point to bless the other person, and rejoice in his prosperity and success; when you do, you bless and prosper yourself.

If you go into the bank, and you see your compet-itor across the street deposit twenty times more than you do, or you see him deposit ten thousand dollars, rejoice and be exceedingly glad to see God's abundance being manifested through one of his sons. You are then blessing and exalting what you are praying for. What you bless, you multiply. What you condemn, you lose.

If you are working in a large organization, and you are silently thinking and resenting the fact you are underpaid, that you are not appreciated, and that you deserve more money and greater recognition, you are subconsciously severing your ties with that organiza-tion. You are setting a law in motion; then the superin-tendent or manager says to you, "We have to let you go." You dismissed yourself. The manager was simply the instrument through which your own negative, mental state was confirmed. In other words he was a messenger telling you what you conceived as true about yourself. It was an example of the law of action and reaction. The action was the internal movement of your mind; the reaction was the response of the outer world to conform to your inner thinking.

Perhaps as you read this, you are thinking of someone who has prospered financially by taking advantage of others, by defrauding them, in selling them unsound investments in property, etc. The answer to this is obvious, because if we rob, cheat, or defraud another, we do the same to ourselves. In reality in this case we are actually hurting or robbing from ourselves. We are in a mood of lack in the first place, which is bound to attract loss to us. The loss may come in many ways; it may come in loss of health, prestige, peace of mind, social status, sickness in the home, or in business. It may not necessarily come in loss of money. We must not be shortsighted and think that the loss has to come just in dollars and cents.

Isn't it a wonderful feeling to place your head on the pillow at night, and feel you are at peace with the whole world, and that your heart is full of goodwill toward all? There are some people who have accumulated money the wrong way, as by tramping on others, trickery, deceit, and chicanery. What is the price? Sometimes it is mental and physical disease, guilt complexes, insomnia, or hidden fears. As one man said to me, "Yes, I rode roughshod over others. I got what I wanted, but

I got cancer doing it." He realized he had attained his wealth in the wrong way.

You can be wealthy and prosperous without hurting anyone. Many men are constantly robbing themselves; they steal from themselves: peace of mind, health, joy, inspiration, happiness, and the laughter of God. They may say that they have never stolen, but is it true? Every time we resent another, or are jealous, or envious of another's wealth or success, we are stealing from ourselves. These are the thieves and robbers which Jesus cast out of the temple; likewise you must cast them out incisively and decisively. Do not let them live in your mind. Cut their heads off with the fire of right thought and feeling.

I remember in the early days of the war reading about a woman in Brooklyn, New York, who went around from store to store buying up all the coffee she could. She knew it was going to be rationed; she was full of fear that there would not be enough for her. She bought as much as she could, and stored it in the cellar. That evening she went to church services. When she came home, burglars had broken down the door, stolen not only the coffee, but silverware, money, jewelry, and other things.

This good woman said what they all say: "Why did this happen to me when I was at church? I never stole from anyone."

Is this true? Was she not in the consciousness of lack and fear when she began to hoard supplies of coffee? Her mood and fear of lack was sufficient to bring about loss in her home and possessions. She did not have to put her hand on the cash register or rob a bank; her fear of lack produced lack. This is the reason that many people who are what society calls "good citizens" suffer loss. They are good in the worldly sense; i.e., they pay their taxes; they obey the laws, vote regularly, and are generous to charities, but they are resentful of others' possessions, their wealth, or social position. If they would like to take money when no one was looking, such an attitude is definitely and positively a state of lack, and may cause the person who indulges in such a mental state to attract charlatans or knaves who may swindle or cheat them in some business transaction.

Before the outer thief robs us, we have first robbed ourselves. There must be an inner thief, before the outer one appears.

A man can have a guilt complex, and be accusing himself constantly. I knew such a man; he was very honest as a teller in a bank. He never stole any money, but he had an illicit romance; he was supporting another woman, and denying his family. He lived in fear that he would be discovered; a deep sense of guilt resulted. Fear follows guilt. Fear causes a contraction of the muscles and mucous membranes; acute sinusitis developed. Medication only gave him temporary relief.

I explained to this client the cause of his trouble, and told him the cure was to give up his outside affair. He said he couldn't; she was his soul mate, and that he had tried. He was always condemning and accusing himself.

One day he was accused by one of the officials of the bank of having embezzled some money; it looked serious for him, as the evidence was circumstantial. He became panic stricken, and realized that the only reason he was wrongfully accused was that he had been accusing and condemning himself. He saw how mind operates. Inasmuch as he was always accusing himself on the inner plane, he would be accused on the outer.

He broke off the relationship immediately with the other woman due to the shock of being accused of embezzling, and began to pray for Divine harmony and understanding between himself and the bank official. He began to claim, "There is nothing hidden that is not revealed. The peace of God reigns supreme in the minds and hearts of all concerned."

Truth prevailed. The whole matter was dissolved in the light of truth. Another young man was discovered as the culprit. The bank teller knew that only through prayer was he saved from a jail sentence.

The great law is, "As you would that men should think about you, think you about them in the same manner. As you would that men should feel about you, feel you also about them in like manner."

Say from your heart, "I wish for every man who walks the earth, what I wish for myself. The sincere wish of my heart is, therefore, peace, love, joy, abundance, and God's blessings to all men everywhere." Rejoice and be glad in the progression, advancement, and prosperity of all men. Whatever you claim as true for yourself, claim it for all men everywhere. If you pray for happiness and peace of mind, let your claim be peace and happiness for all. Do not ever try and deprive another of any joy. If you do, you deprive yourself. When the ship comes in for your friend, it comes in for you also.

If someone is promoted in your organization, be glad and happy. Congratulate him, rejoice in his advancement and recognition. If you are angry or resentful, you are demoting yourself. Do not try and withhold from another his God-given birthright to happiness, success, achievement, abundance, and all good things.

Jesus said, "Sow up for yourselves treasures in heaven, where the moth and the rust doth not consume, and where thieves cannot break through and steal." Hatred and resentment rot and corrode the heart causing us to become full of scars, impurities, toxins, and poisons.

The treasures of heaven are the truths of God which we possess in our soul. Fill your minds with peace, harmony, faith, joy, honesty, integrity, loving kindness, and gentleness; then you will be sowing for yourself treasures in the heavens of your own mind.

If you are seeking wisdom regarding investments, or if you are worried about your stocks or bonds, quietly claim, "Infinite Intelligence governs and watches over all my financial transactions, and whatsoever I do shall prosper." Do this frequently and you will find that your investments will be wise; moreover you will be protected from loss, as you will be prompted to sell your securities or holdings before any loss accrues to you.

Let the following prayer be used daily by you regarding your home, business, and possessions: "The overshadowing Presence which guides the planets on their course and causes the sun to shine, watches over all my possessions, home, business, and all things that are mine. God is my fortress and vault. All my possessions are secure in God. It is wonderful." By reminding yourself daily of this great truth, and by observing the laws of Love, you will always be guided, watched over, and prospered in all your ways. You will never suffer from loss; for you have chosen the Most High as your Counsellor and Guide. The envelope of God's Love surrounds, enfolds, and encompasses you at all times. You rest in the Everlasting Arms of God.

All of us should seek an inner guidance for our problems. If you have a financial problem, repeat this before you retire at night: "Now I shall sleep in peace. I have turned this matter over to the God-Wisdom within. It knows only the answer. As the sun rises in the morning, so will my answer be resurrected. I know the sunrise never fails." Then go off to sleep.

Do not fret, fuss, and fume over a problem. Night brings counsel. Sleep on it. Your intellect cannot solve all your problems. Pray for the Light that is to come. Remember the dawn always comes; then the shadows flee away. Let your sleep every night be a contented bliss.

You are not a victim of circumstances, except you believe you are. You can rise and overcome any circumstance or condition. You will have different experiences as you stand on the rock of spiritual Truth, steadfast, and faithful to your deeper purposes and desires.

In large stores, the management employs store detectives to prevent people from stealing; they catch a number every day trying to get something for nothing. All such people are living in the consciousness of lack and limitation, and are stealing from themselves, attracting at the same time all manner of loss. These people lack faith in God, and the understanding of how their minds work. If they would pray for true peace, Divine expression, and supply, they would find work; then by honesty, integrity, and perseverance they would become a credit to themselves and society at large.

Jesus said, "For ye have the poor always with you; but me ye have not always." The *poor states* of consciousness are always with us in this sense, that no matter how much wealth you now have, there is something you want with all your heart. It may be a problem of health; perhaps a son or daughter needs guidance, or harmony is lacking in the home. At that moment you are poor.

We could not know what abundance was, except we were conscious of lack. "I have chosen twelve, and one of you is a devil."

Whether it be the king of England or the boy in the slums, we are all born into limitation and into the race belief. It is through these limitations we grow. We could never discover the Inner Power, except through problems and difficulties; these are our *poor states* which prod us in seeking the solution. We could not know what joy was, except we could shed a tear of sorrow. We must be aware of poverty, to seek liberation and freedom, and ascend into God's opulence.

The *poor states*, such as fear, ignorance, worry, lack, and pain are not bad when they cause you to seek the opposite. When you get into trouble, and get kicked around from pillar to post; when you ask negative, heart-rending questions, such as "Why are all these things happening to me?" "Why does there seem to be a jinx following me?" light will come into your mind. Through your suffering, pain, or misery, you will discover the truth which sets you free. "Sweet are the uses of adversity, like a toad ugly and venomous, yet wears a precious jewel on its head."

Through dissatisfaction we are led to satisfaction. All those studying the laws of life have been dissatisfied with something. They have had some problem or difficulty which they could not solve; or they were not satisfied with the man-made answers to life's riddles. They have found their answer in the God-Presence within themselves—the pearl of great price—the precious jewel. The Bible says, "I sought the Lord, and I found him, and He delivered me from all my fears."

When you realize your ambition or desire, you will be satisfied for only a period of brief time; then the urge to expand will come again. This is Life seeking to express Itself at higher levels through you. When one desire is satisfied, another comes, etc. to infinity. You are here to grow. Life is progression; it is not static. You are here to go from glory to glory; there is no end; for there is no end to God's glory.

We are all poor in the sense we are forever seeking more light, wisdom, happiness, and greater joy out of life. God is Infinite, and never in Eternity could you exhaust the glory, beauty, and wisdom which is within; this is how wonderful you are.

In the absolute state all things are finished, but in the relative world we must awaken to that glory which was ours before the world was. No matter how wise you are, you are seeking more wisdom; so you are still poor. No matter how intelligent you are in the field of mathematics, physics, or astronomy, you are only scratching the surface. You are still poor. The journey is ever onward, upward, and Godward. It is really an awakening process, whereby you realize creation is finished. When you know God does not have to learn, grow, expand, or unfold, you begin to gradually awaken from the dream of limitation, and become alive in God. As the scales of fear, ignorance, race belief, and mass hypnosis fall from your eyes, you begin to see as God sees. The blind spots are removed; then you begin to see the world as God made it; for we begin to see it through God's eyes. Now you say, "Behold, the Kingdom of Heaven is at hand!"

Feed the "poor" within you; clothe the naked ideas, and give them form by believing in the reality of the idea, trusting the great Fabricator within to clothe it in form and objectify it. Now your word (idea) shall become flesh (take form). When you are hungry (poor states), you seek food. When worried, you seek peace. When you are sick, you seek health; when you are weak, you seek strength. Your desire for prosperity is the voice of God in you telling you that abundance is yours; therefore, through your poor state, you find the urge to grow, to expand, to unfold, to achieve, and to accomplish your desires.

A pain in your shoulder is a blessing in disguise; it tells you to do something about it at once. If there were no pain and no indication of trouble, your arm might fall off on the street. Your pain is God's alarm system telling you to seek His Peace and His Healing Power, and move from darkness to Light. When cold, you build a fire. When you are hungry, you eat. When you are in lack, enter into the mood of opulence and plenty. Imagine the end; rejoice in it. Having imagined the end, and felt it as true, you have willed the means to the realization of the end.

When you are fearful and worried, feed your mind with the great truths of God that have stood the test of time and will last forever. You can receive comfort by meditating on the great psalms. For example: "The Lord is my shepherd; I shall not want." "God is my refuge, my salvation, whom shall I fear?" "God is an ever-present help in time of trouble." "My God in Him will I trust." "He shall cover me with His feathers, and under His wings shall I rest." "One with God is a majority." "If God be for me, who can be against me?" "I do all things through Christ which strengtheneth me." Let the healing vibrations of these truths flood your mind and heart; then you will crowd out of your mind all your fears, doubts, and worries through this meditative process.

Imbibe another great spiritual truth: "A merry heart maketh a cheerful countenance." "A merry heart hath a continual feast." "A merry heart doeth good like a medicine; a broken spirit drieth the bones." "Therefore I put thee in remembrance that thou stir up the gift of God within thee." Begin now to stir up the gift of God by completely rejecting the evidence of senses, the tyranny and despotism of the race mind, and give complete recognition to the spiritual Power within you as the only Cause, the only Power, and the only Presence. Know that it is a responsive and beneficent Power. "Draw nigh unto it, and it will draw nigh unto you." Turn to It devotedly with assurance, trust, and love; it will respond to you as love, peace, guidance, and prosperity.

It will be your Comforter, Guide, Counsellor, and your heavenly Father. You will then say, "God is Love. I have found Him, and He truly has delivered me from all my fears." Furthermore, you will find yourself in green pastures, where abundance and all of God's riches flow freely through you.

Say to yourself freely and joyously during the day, "I walk in the consciousness of the Presence of God all day long." "His fullness flows through me at all times filling up all the empty vessels in my life."

When you are filled full of the feeling of being what you long to be, your prayer is answered. Are all the vessels full in your life? Look under health, wealth, love, and expression. Are you fully satisfied on all levels? Is there something lacking in one of these four? All that you seek, no matter what it is, comes under one of these classifications.

If you say, "All I want is truth or wisdom," you are expressing the desire of all men everywhere. That is what everyone wants, even though he or she may word it differently. Truth or wisdom is the overall desire of every man; this comes under the classification of expression. You wish to express more and more of God here and now.

Through your lack, limitation, and problems, you grow in God's Light, and you discover yourself. There is no other way whereby you could discover yourself.

If you could not use your powers two ways, you would never discover yourself; neither would you ever deduce a law governing you. If you were compelled to be good, or compelled to love, that would not be love. You would then be an automaton. You have freedom to love, because you can give it, or retain it. If compelled to love, there is no love. Aren't you flattered when some woman tells you she loves you and wants you? She has chosen you from all the men in the world. She does not have to love you. If she were forced to love you, you would not be flattered or happy about it.

You have freedom to be a murderer or a Holy man. This is the reason that we praise such men as Lincoln and others. They decided to choose the good; we praise them for their choice. If we believe that circumstances, conditions, events, age, race, religious training, or early environment can preclude the possibility of our attaining a happy, prosperous life, we are thieves and robbers. All that is necessary to express happiness and prosperity is to feel happy and prosperous. The feeling of wealth produces wealth. States of consciousness manifest themselves. This is why it is said, "All that ever came before me (feeling) are thieves and robbers." Feeling is the law, and the law is the feeling.

Your desire for prosperity is really the promise of God saying that His riches are yours; accept this promise without any mental reservation.

Quimby likened prayer to that of a lawyer pleading the case before the judge. This teacher of the laws of mind said he could prove the defendant was not guilty as charged, but that the person was a victim of lies and false beliefs. You are the judge; you render your own verdict; then you are set free. The negative thoughts of lack, poverty, and failure are all false; they are all lies; there is nothing to back them up.

You know there is only one spiritual Power, one primal cause, and you, therefore, cease giving power to conditions, circumstances, and opinions of men. Give all Power to the Spiritual Power within you, knowing that It will respond to your thought of abundance and prosperity. Recognizing the supremacy of the Spirit within, and the Power of your own thought or mental image is the way to opulence, freedom, and constant supply. Accept the abundant life in your own mind. Your mental acceptance and expectancy of wealth has its own mathematics and mechanics of expression. As you enter into the mood of opulence, all things necessary for the abundant life will come to pass. You are now the judge arriving at a decision in the courthouse of your mind. You have, like Quimby, produced indisputable evidence showing how the laws of your mind work, and you are now free from fear. You have executed and chopped the heads off all the fear and superstitious thoughts in your mind. Fear is the signal for action; it is not really bad; it tells you to move to the opposite which is faith in God and all positive values.

Let this be your daily prayer; write it in your heart: "God is the source of my supply. That supply is my supply now. His riches flow to me freely, copiously, and abundantly. I am forever conscious of my true worth. I give of my talents freely, and I am wonderfully, divinely compensated. Thank you, Father!"

Chapter Two

The Road to Riches

Riches are of the mind. Let us suppose for a moment that a physician's diploma was stolen together with his office equipment. I am sure you would agree that his wealth was in his mind. He could still carry on, diagnose disease, prescribe, operate, and lecture on materia medica. Only his symbols were stolen; he could always get additional supplies. His riches were in his mental capacity, knowledge to help others, and his ability to contribute to humanity in general.

You will always be wealthy when you have an intense desire to contribute to the good of mankind.

Your urge for service—i.e., to give of your talents to the world—will always find a response in the heart of the universe.

I knew a man in New York during the financial crisis of 1929, who lost everything he had including his home and all his life's savings. I met him after a lecture which I had given at one of the hotels in the city. This was what he said: "I lost everything. I made a million dollars in four years. I will make it again. All I have lost is a symbol. I can again attract the symbol of wealth in the same way as honey attracts flies."

I followed the career of this man for several years to discover the key to his success. The key may seem strange to you; yet it is a very old one. The name he gave the key was, "Change water into wine!" He read this passage in the Bible, and he knew it was the answer to perfect health, happiness, peace of mind, and prosperity.

Wine in the Bible always means the realization of your desires, urges, plans, dreams, propositions, etc.; in other words, it is the things you wish to accomplish, achieve, and bring forth.

Water in the Bible usually refers to your mind or consciousness. Water takes the shape of any vessel into which it is poured; likewise whatever you feel and believe as true will become manifest in your world; thus you are always changing water into wine.

The Bible was written by illumined men; it teaches practical, everyday psychology and a way of life. One of the cardinal tenets of the Bible is that you determine, mold, fashion, and shape your own destiny through right thought, feeling, and beliefs. It teaches you that you can solve any problem, overcome any situation, and that you are born to succeed, to win, and to triumph. In order to discover the Royal Road to Riches, and receive the strength and security necessary to advance in life, you must cease viewing the Bible in the traditional way.

The above man who was in a financial crisis used to say to himself frequently during the days when he was without funds, "I can change water into wine!" These words meant to him, "I can exchange the poverty ideas in my mind for the realization of my present desires or needs which are wealth and financial supply."

His mental attitude (water) was, "Once I made a fortune honestly. I will make it again (wine)." His regular affirmation consisted of, "I attracted the symbol (money) once, I am attracting it again. I know this, and feel it is true (wine)." This man went to work as a salesman for a chemical organization. Ideas for the better promotion of their products came to him; he passed them on to his organization. It was not long until he became vice president. Within four years the company made him president. His constant mental attitude was, "I can change water into wine!"

Look upon the story in John of changing water into wine in a figurative way, and say to yourself as the above-mentioned chemical salesman did: "I can make the invisible ideas, urges, dreams, and desires of mine visible, because I have discovered a simple, universal law of mind."

The law he demonstrated is the law of action and reaction. It means your external world, body, circumstances, environment, and financial status are always a perfect reflection of your inner thinking, beliefs, feelings, and convictions. This being true, you can now change your inner pattern of thought by dwelling on the idea of success, wealth, and peace of mind. As you busy your mind with these latter concepts, these ideas will gradually seep into your mentality like seeds planted in the ground. As all seeds (thoughts and ideas) grow after their kind, so will your habitual thinking and feeling manifest in prosperity, success, and peace of mind. Wise thought (action) is followed by right action (reaction).

You can acquire riches when you become aware of the fact that prayer is a marriage feast. The *feast* is a psychological one; you meditate (mentally eat of) on your good or your desire until you become *one* with it.

I will now cite a case history from my files relating how a young girl performed her first miracle in transforming "water into wine." She operated a very beautiful hair salon. Her mother became ill, and she had to devote considerable time at home neglecting her business. During her absence two of her assistants embezzled funds. She was forced into bankruptcy, losing her home and finding herself deeply in debt. She was unable to pay hospital bills for her mother, and she was now unemployed.

I explained to this woman the magic formula of changing water into wine. Again we made it clear to her that wine means answered prayer or the objectification of her ideal.

She was quarreling with the outside world. She said, "Look at the facts: I have lost everything; it is a cruel world. I cannot pay my bills. I do not pray; for I have lost hope." She was so absorbed and engrossed in the material world, that she was completely oblivious to the internal cause of her situation. As we talked, she began to understand that she had to resolve the quarrel in her mind.

No matter what your desire or ideal is as you read this book, you will also find some thought or idea in your mind opposed to it. For example your desire may be for health; perhaps there are several thoughts such as these in your mind simultaneously: "I can't be healed. I have tried, but it is no use; it's getting worse." "I don't know enough about spiritual mind healing."

As you study yourself, don't you have a tug of war in your mind? Like this girl, you find environment and external affairs challenging your desire of expression, wealth, and peace of mind.

True prayer is a mental marriage feast, and it teaches us all how to resolve the mental conflict. In prayer you "write" what you *believe* in your own mind. Emerson said, "A man is what he thinks about all day long." By your habitual thinking you make your own mental laws of belief. By repeating a certain train of thought you establish definite opinions and beliefs in the deeper mind called the subconscious; then such mental acceptances, beliefs, and opinions direct and control all the outer actions. To understand this and begin to apply it is the first step in changing "water into wine," or changing lack and limitation into abundance and opulence. The man who is unaware of his own inner, spiritual powers is, therefore, subject to race beliefs, lack, and limitation.

Open your Bible now, and perform your first miracle, as this beauty operator did. You can do it. If you merely read the Bible as a historical event, you will miss the spiritual, mental, scientific view of the laws of mind with which we are concerned in this book.

Let us take this passage: "And the third day there was a marriage in Cana of Galilea; and the mother of Jesus was there." *Galilee* means your mind or consciousness. *Cana* means your desire. The *marriage* is purely mental or the subjective embodiment of your desire. This whole, beautiful drama of prayer is a psychological one in which all the characters are mental states, feelings, and ideas within you.

One of the meanings of *Jesus* is illumined reason. The *mother of Jesus* means the feeling, moods, or emotions which possess us.

"And both Jesus was called, and his disciples, to the marriage." *Your disciples* are your inner powers and faculties enabling you to realize your desires.

"And when they wanted wine, the mother of Jesus saith unto him, They have no wine." *Wine*, as we have stated, represents the answered prayer or the manifestation of your desire and ideals in life. You can now see this is an everyday drama taking place in your own life.

When you wish to accomplish something as this girl did, namely, finding work, supply, and a way out of your problem, suggestions of lack come to you; such as, "There is no hope. All is lost, I can't accomplish it; it is hopeless." This is the voice from the outside world saying to you, "They have no wine," or "Look at the facts." This is your feeling of lack, limitation, or bondage speaking.

How do you meet the challenge of circumstances and conditions? By now you are getting acquainted with the laws of mind which are as follows: "As I think and feel inside, so is my outside world; i.e., my body, finances, environment, social position, and all phases of my external relationship to the world and man." Your internal, mental movements and imagery govern, control, and direct the external plane in your life.

The Bible says, "As he thinketh in his heart, so *is* he." The *heart* is a Chaldean word meaning the subconscious mind. In other words your thought must reach subjective levels by engaging the power of your subliminal self.

Thought and feeling are your destiny. Thought charged with feeling and interest is always subjectified, and becomes manifest in your world. *Prayer* is a marriage of thought and feeling, or your idea and emotion; this is what the marriage feast relates.

Any idea or desire of the mind felt as true comes to pass, whether it is good, bad, or indifferent. Knowing the law now that what you imagine and feel in your mind, you will express, manifest, or experience in the outside, enables you to begin to discipline your mind.

When the suggestion of lack, fear, doubt, or despair (they have no wine) come to your mind, immediately reject it mentally by focusing your attention at once on the answered prayer, or the fulfillment of your desire.

The statement given in the Bible from John 2, "Mine hour is not yet come," and "Woman, what have I to do with thee," are figurative, idiomatic, oriental expressions.

As we paraphrase this quotation, *woman* means the negative feeling that you indulge in. These negative suggestions have no power or reality, because there is nothing to back them up.

A suggestion of lack has no power; the power is resident in your own thought and feeling.

What does God mean to you? *God* is the Name given to the One Spiritual Power. *God* is the One Invisible Source from Which all things flow.

When your thoughts are constructive and harmonious, the spiritual power being responsive to your thought flows as harmony, health, and abundance. Practice the wonderful discipline of completely rejecting every thought of lack by immediately recognizing the availability of the spiritual power, and its response to your constructive thoughts and imagery; then you will be practicing the truth found in these words, "Woman what have I to do with thee?"

We read, "Mine hour is not yet come." This means that while you have not yet reached a conviction or positive state of mind, you know you are on the way mentally, because you are engaging your mind on the positive ideals, goals, and objectives in life. Whatever the mind dwells upon, it multiplies, magnifies, and causes it to grow until finally the mind becomes qualified with the new state of consciousness. You are then conditioned positively, whereas before you were conditioned negatively.

The spiritual man in prayer moves from the mood of lack to the mood of confidence, peace, and trust in the spiritual power within himself. Since his trust and faith are in the Spiritual Power, his mother (moods and feeling) registers a feeling of triumph or victory; this will bring about the solution or the answer to your prayer.

The waterpots in the story from the Bible refer to the mental cycles that man goes through in order to bring about the subjective realization of his desire. The length of time may be a moment, hour, week, or month depending on the faith and state of consciousness of the student.

In prayer we must cleanse our mind of false beliefs, fear, doubt, and anxiety by becoming completely detached from the evidence of senses and the external world. In the peacefulness and quietude of your mind, wherein you have stilled the wheels of your mind, meditate on the joy of the answered prayer until that inner certitude comes, whereby *you know that you know*. When you have succeeded in being one with your desire, you have succeeded in the mental marriage—or the union of your feeling with your idea.

I am sure you wish to be married (one with) to health, harmony, success, and achievement in your mind at this moment. Every time you pray you are trying to perform the *marriage feast of Cana* (realization of your desire or ideas). You want to be mentally identified with the concept of peace, success, wellbeing, and perfect health.

"They filled them up to the brim." *The six waterpots* represent your own mind in the spiritual and mental creative act. You must fill your mind *to the brim*, meaning you must become filled full of the feeling of being what you long to be. When you succeed in filling your mind with the ideal you wish to accomplish or express, you are full to the brim; then you cease praying about it; for you feel its reality in your mind. You *know*! It is a finished state of consciousness. You are at peace about it.

"And he saith unto them Draw out now, and bear unto the governor of the feast." Whatever is impregnated in our subconscious mind is always objectified on the screen of space; consequently when we enter a state of conviction that our prayer is answered, we have given the command, "Bear unto the governor of the feast."

You are always governing your mental feast. During the day thousands of thoughts, suggestions, opinions, sights, and sounds reach your eyes and ears. You can reject them as unfit for mental consumption or entertain them as you choose. Your conscious, reasoning, intellectual mind is the governor of the feast. When you consciously choose to entertain, meditate, feast upon, and imagine your heart's desire as true, it becomes a living embodiment, and a part of your mentality, so that your deeper self gives birth or expression to it. In other words what is impressed subjectively is expressed objectively. Your senses or conscious mind sees the objectification of your good. When the conscious mind becomes aware of "water made into wine," it becomes aware of the answered prayer. *Water* might be called, also, the invisible, formless, spiritual power, unconditioned consciousness. *Wine* is conditioned consciousness, or the mind giving birth to its beliefs and convictions.

The servants which draw the water for you represent the mood of peace, confidence, and faith. According to your faith or feeling, your good is attracted or drawn to you.

Imbibe, cherish, fall in love with these spiritual principles which are discussed in this book. In the first recorded miracle of Jesus, you are told that prayer is a marriage feast, or the mind uniting with its desire.

Love is the fulfilling of the law. Love is really an emotional attachment, a sense of oneness with your good. You must be true to that which you love. You must be loyal to your purpose or to your ideal. We are not being true to the one we love, when we are flirting or mentally entertaining other marriages with fear, doubt, worry, anxiety, or false beliefs. Love is a state of oneness, a state of fulfillment. (Refer to the book by the author, *Love is Freedom*.)

When this simple drama was explained to the beauty operator mentioned about, she became rich mentally. She understood this drama, and she put it into practice in her life. This is how she prayed: She knew that the water (her own mind) would flow, and fill up all the *empty vessels* in response to her new way of thinking and feeling.

At night this client became very quiet and still, relaxed her body, and began to use constructive imagery. The steps she used are as follows:

First step: She began to imagine the local bank manager was congratulating her on her wonderful deposits in the bank. She kept imagining that for about five minutes.

The second step: In her imagination she heard her mother saying to her, "I am so happy about your wonderful, new position." She continued to hear her say this in a happy, joyous way for about three to five minutes.

The third step: Vividly she imagined the writer was in front of her performing her marriage ceremony. This woman heard me saying as the officiating minister, "I now pronounce you man and wife." Completing this routine, she went off to sleep feeling filled full, i.e., sensing and feeling within herself the joy of the answered prayer.

Nothing happened for three weeks; in fact things got much worse, but she persevered, refusing to take "No" for her answer. She knew that in order to grow spiritually, she too, had to perform her first miracle by changing her fear to faith, her mood of lack to a mood of opulence and prosperity, by changing consciousness (water) into the conditions, circumstances, and experiences she wished to express.

Consciousness, Awareness, Beingness, Principle, Spirit, or whatever Name you give It is the cause of all; it is the only Presence and Power. The Spiritual Power of Spirit within us is the cause and substance of all things. All things—birds, trees, stars, sun, moon, earth, gold, silver, and platinum—are its manifestations. It is the cause and substance of all things. "There is none else."

Understanding this she knew that *water* (consciousness) could become supply in the form of money, true place, or true expression for herself, health for her mother, as well as companionship and fullness of life. She saw this simple—yet profound—truth in the twinkling of an eye, and said to me, "I *accept* my good."

She knew that nothing is hidden from us; all of God is within us, waiting for our discovery and inquiry.

In less than a month this young girl got married. The writer performed the ceremony. I pronounced the words she heard me say over and over again in her meditative, relaxed state, "I now pronounce you man and wife!"

Her husband gave her a check for $24,000 as a wedding present, as well as a trip around the world. Her new expression as a beauty operator was to beautify her home and garden, and make the desert of her mind rejoice and blossom as the rose.

She changed "water into wine." *Water* or her consciousness became charged or conditioned by her constant, true, happy imagery. These images, when sustained regularly, systematically, and with faith in the developing powers of the deeper mind, will come out of the darkness (subconscious mind) into light (objectified on the screen of space).

There is one important rule: Do not expose this newly developed film to the shattering light of fear, doubt, despondency, and worry. Whenever worry or fear knocks at your door, immediately turn to the picture you developed in your mind, and say to yourself, "A beautiful picture is being developed now in the dark house of my mind." Mentally pour on that picture your feeling of joy, faith, and understanding. You know you have operated a psychological, spiritual law; for what is impressed shall be expressed. It is wonderful!

The following is a sure, certain way for developing and manifesting all the material riches and supply you need all the days of your life. If you apply this formula sincerely and honestly, you should be amply rewarded on the external plane. I will illustrate this by telling you of a man who came to see me in London in desperate financial straits. He was a member of the Church of England, and had studied the working of the subconscious mind to some extent.

I told him to say frequently during the day, "God is the source of my supply, and all my needs are met at every moment of time and point of space." Think also of all the animal life in this world, and in all the galaxies of space which are now being taken care of by an Infinite Intelligence. Notice how nature is lavish, extravagant, and bountiful. Think of the fish of the sea which are all being sustained, as well as the birds of the air!"

He began to realize that since he was born, he had been taken care of; fed by his mother; clothed by his father, and watched over by tender, loving parents. This man got a job and was paid in a wonderful way. He reasoned that it was illogical to assume that the Principle of Life which gave him life, and always took care of him would suddenly cease to respond to him.

He realized that he had cut off his own supply by resenting his employer, self-condemnation, criticism of himself, and by his own sense of unworthiness. He had psychologically severed the cord which joined him to the Infinite Source of all things—the Indwelling Spirit or Life Principle, called by some "Consciousness or Awareness."

Man is not fed like the birds; he must consciously commune with the Indwelling Power and Presence, and receive guidance, strength, vitality, and all things necessary for the fulfillment of his needs.

This is the formula which he used to change water into the wine of abundance and financial success. He realized God or the Spiritual Power within him was the cause of all; furthermore he realized that if he could sell himself the idea that wealth was his by Divine right, he would manifest abundance of supply.

The affirmation he used was, "God is the source of my supply. All my financial and other needs are met at every moment of time and point of space; there is always a divine surplus." This simple statement repeated frequently, knowingly, and intelligently conditioned his mind to a prosperity consciousness.

All he had to do was to sell himself this positive idea, in the same way a good salesman has to sell himself on the merits of his product. Such a person is convinced of the integrity of his company, the high quality of the product, the good service which it will give the customer, and the fact that the price is right, etc.

I told him whenever negative thoughts came to his mind, which would happen, not to fight them, quarrel with them in any way, but simply go back to the spiritual, mental formula, and repeat it quietly and lovingly to himself. Negative thoughts came to him in avalanches at times in the form of a flood of negativity. Each time he met them with the positive, firm, loyal conviction: "God supplies all my needs; there is a Divine surplus in my life."

He said as he drove his car, and went through his day's routine, that a host of sundry, miscellaneous, negative concepts crowded his mind from time to time; such as, "There is no hope." "You are broke." Each time such negative thoughts came, he refused their mental admission by turning to the Eternal Source of wealth, health, and all things which he knew to be his own spiritual awareness. Definitely and positively he claimed, "God is the source of my supply, and that supply is mine now!" Or, "There is a Divine solution. God's wealth is my wealth," and other affirmative, positive statements which charged his mind with hope, faith, expectancy, and ultimately a conviction in an ever-flowing fountain of riches supplying all his needs copiously, joyously, and endlessly.

The negative flood of thoughts came to him as often as fifty times in an hour; each time he refused to open the door of his mind to these gangsters, assassins, and thieves which he knew would only rob him of peace, wealth, success, and all good things. Instead he opened the door of his mind to the idea of God's Eternal Life Principle of supply flowing through him as wealth, health, energy, power, and all things necessary to lead a full and happy life here.

As he continued to do this, the second day not so many thieves knocked at his door; the third day, the flow of negative visitors was less; the fourth day, they came intermittently, hoping for admission, but receiving the same mental response: "No entrance! I accept only thoughts and concepts which activate, heal, bless, and inspire my mind!"

He reconditioned his consciousness or mind to a wealth consciousness. "The prince of this world cometh, and hath nothing in me"—This conveys to your mind: The negative thoughts, such as, fear, lack, worry, anxiety came, but they received no response from his mind. He was now immune; God intoxicated, and seized by a divine faith in an ever-expanding consciousness of abundance and financial supply. This man did not lose everything; neither did he go into bankruptcy; he was given extended credit; his business improved; new doors opened up, and he prospered.

Remember always in the prayer-process, you must be loyal to your ideal, purpose, and objective. Many people fail to realize wealth and financial success, because they pray two ways. They affirm God is their supply, and that they are divinely prospered, but a few minutes later they deny their good by saying, "I can't pay this bill." "I can't afford this, that, or the other things." Or they say to themselves, "A jinx is following me." "I can't ever make ends meet." "I never have enough to go around." All such statements are highly destructive, and neutralize your positive prayers. This is what is called, "praying two ways."

You must be faithful to your plan or your goal. You must be true to your knowledge of the spiritual power. Cease making negative marriages, i.e., uniting with negative thoughts, fears, and worries.

Prayer is like a captain directing the course of his ship. You must have a destination. You must know where you are going. The captain of the ship, knowing the laws of navigation, regulates his course accordingly. If the ship is turned from its course by storms or unruly waves, he calmly redirects it along its true course.

You are the captain on the bridge, and you are giving the orders in the way of thoughts, feelings, opinions, beliefs, moods, and mental tones. Keep your eye on the beam. *You go where your vision is!* Cease, therefore, looking at all the obstacles, delays, and impediments that would cause you to go off your course. Be definite and positive. Decide where you are going. Know that your mental attitude is the ship which will take you from the mood of lack and limitation, to the mood and feeling of opulence, and to the belief in the inevitable law of God working for you.

Quimby, who was a doctor, a wonderful student, and teacher of the mental and spiritual laws of mind, said, "Man acts as he is acted upon." What moves you now? What is it that determines your response to life? The answer is as follows: Your ideas, beliefs, and opinions activate your mind and condition you to the point that you become, as Quimby stated, "An expression of your beliefs." This illustrates the truth of Quimby's statement: "Man is belief expressed."

Another popular statement of Quimby's was, "Our minds mingle like atmospheres, and each person has his identity in that atmosphere." When you were a child, you were subject to the moods, feelings, beliefs, and the general mental atmosphere of the home. The fears, anxieties, superstitions, as well as the religious faith and convictions of the parents were impressed on your mind.

Let us say the child had been brought up in a poverty-stricken home, in which there was never enough to go around, financially speaking; he heard constantly the complaint of lack and limitation.

You could say, like Salter in his conditioned reflex therapy, that the child was conditioned to poverty. The young man may have a poverty complex based on his early experiences, training, and beliefs, but he can rise above any situation, and become free; this is done through the power of prayer.

I knew a young boy aged 17, who was born in a place called Hell's Kitchen, in New York. He listened to some lectures I was giving in Steinway Hall, New York, at the time. This boy realized that he had been the victim of negative, destructive thinking, and that if he did not redirect his mind along constructive channels, the world-mind with its fears, failures, hates, and jealousies would move in and control him. "Man acts as he is acted upon."

It stands to reason, as Quimby knew, that if man will not take charge of his own house (mind), the propaganda, false beliefs, fears, and worries of the phenomenalistic world will act as a hypnotic spell over him.

We are immersed in the race mind which believes in sickness, death, misfortune, accident, failures, disease, and diverse disasters. Follow the Biblical injunc-

tion: "Come out from among them, and be separate."
Identify yourself mentally and emotionally with the
Eternal Verities which have stood the test of time.

This young man decided to think and plan for
himself. He decided to take the Royal Road to Riches
by accepting God's abundance here and now, and to fill
his mind with spiritual concepts and perceptions. He
knew, as he did this, he would automatically crowd out
of his mind all negative patterns.

He adopted a simple process called, "scientific
imagination." He had a wonderful voice, but it was
not cultivated or developed. I told him the image he
gave attention to in his mind would be developed in his
deeper mind and come to pass. He understood this to
be a law of mind—a law of action and reaction—i.e.,
the response of the deeper mind to the mental picture
held in the conscious mind.

This young man would sit down quietly in his
room at home; relax his whole body, and vividly imagine himself singing before a microphone. He would actually reach out for the "feel" of the instrument. He
would hear me congratulate him on his wonderful contract, and tell him how magnificent his voice was. By
giving his attention and devotion to this mental image
regularly and systematically, a deep impression was
made on his subconscious mind.

A short time elapsed, and an Italian voice instructor in New York gave him free lessons several times a week, because he saw his possibilities. He got a contract which sent him abroad to sing in the salons of Europe, Asia, South Africa, and other places. His financial worries were over; for he also received a wonderful salary. His hidden talents and ability to release them were his real riches. These talents and powers within all of us are God-given; let us release them.

Did you ever say to yourself, "How can I be more useful to my fellow creature?" "How can I contribute more to humanity?"

A minister-friend of mine told me that in his early days he and his church suffered financially. His technique or process was this simple prayer which worked wonders for him, "God reveals to me better ways to present the truths of God to my fellow creature." Money poured in; the mortgage was paid in a few years, and he has never worried about money since.

As you read this chapter, you have now learned that the inner feelings, moods, and beliefs of man always control and govern his external world. The inner movements of the mind control the outer movements. To change the outside, you must change the inside. "As in Heaven, so on earth;" or as in my mind or consciousness, so is it in my body, circumstances, and environment.

The Bible says, "There is nothing hidden that shall not be revealed." For example if you are sick, you are revealing a mental and emotional pattern which is the cause. If you are upset, or if you receive tragic news, notice how you reveal it in your face, eyes, gestures, tonal qualities, also in your gait and posture. As a matter of fact your whole body reveals your inner distress. You could, of course, through mental discipline and prayer, remain absolutely poised, serene, and calm, refusing to betray your hidden feelings or mental states. You could order the muscles of your body to relax, be quiet, and be still; they would have to obey you. Your eyes, face, and lips would not betray any sign of grief, anger, or despondency. On the other hand with a little discipline, through prayer and meditation, you could reverse the entire picture. Even though you had received disturbing news, regardless of its grave nature, you could show and exhibit joy, peace, relaxation, and a vibrant, buoyant nature. No one would ever know that you were the recipient of so-called bad news.

Regardless of what kind of news you received today, you could go to the mirror, look at your face, lips, eyes, and your gestures, as you tell yourself, and imagine you have heard the news of having received a vast fortune. Dramatize it, feel it, thrill to it, and notice how your whole body responds to the inner thrill.

You can reverse any situation through prayer. Busy your mind with the concepts of peace, success, wealth, and happiness. Identify yourself with these ideas mentally, emotionally, and pictorially.

Get a picture of yourself as you want to be; retain that image; sustain it with joy, faith, and expectancy; finally you will succeed in experiencing its manifestation.

I say to people who consult me regarding financial lack to "marry wealth." Some see the point, others do not. As all Bible students know, your wife is what you are mentally joined to, united with, or at one with.

In other words what you conceive and believe, you give it conception. If you believe the world is cold, cruel, and harsh, that it is a "dog eat dog" way of life, that is your concept; you are married to it, and you will have children or issue by that marriage. The children from such a mental marriage or belief will be your experiences, conditions, and circumstances together with all other events in your life. All your experiences and reactions to life will be the image and likeness of the ideas which fathered them.

Look at the many wives the average man is living with, such as fear, doubt, anxiety, criticism, jealousy, and anger; these play havoc with his mind. Marry wealth by claiming, feeling, and believing: "God supplies all my needs according to his riches in glory." Or take the following statement, and repeat it over and over again knowingly until your consciousness is conditioned by it, or it becomes a part of your meditation: "I am divinely expressed, and I have a wonderful income." Do not say this in a parrot-like fashion, but know that your train of thought is being engraved in your deeper mind, and it becomes a conditioned state of consciousness. Let the phrase become meaningful to you. Pour life, love, and feeling on it, making it alive.

One of my class-students recently opened a restaurant. He phoned me saying that he got married to a restaurant; he meant that he had made up his mind to be very successful, diligent, and persevering, and to see that his business prospered. This man's *wife* (mental) was his belief in the accomplishment of his desire or wish.

Identify yourself with your aim in life, and cease mental marriages with criticism, self-condemnation, anger, fear, and worry. Give attention to your chosen ideal, being full of faith and confidence in the inevitable law of prosperity and success. You will accomplish nothing by loving your ideal one minute, and denying it the next minute; this is like mixing acid and an alkali; for you will get an inert substance. In going along the Royal Road to Riches, you must be faithful to your chosen ideal (your wife).

We find illustrations in the Bible relating to these same truths. For instance, "Eve came out of Adam's rib." *Your rib* is your concept, desire, idea, plan, goal, or aim in life.

Eve means the emotion, feeling nature, or the inner tone. In other words you must mother the idea. The idea must be mothered, loved, and felt as true, in order to manifest your aim in life.

The *idea* is the father; the *emotion* is the mother; this is the marriage feast which is always taking place in your mind.

Ouspensky spoke of the third element which entered in or was formed following the union of your desire and feeling. He called it the neutral element. We may call it "peace"; for God is Peace.

The Bible says, "And the government shall be on his shoulders." In other words let Divine Wisdom be your guide. Let the subjective Wisdom within you lead, guide, and govern you in all your ways. Turn over your request to this Indwelling Presence knowing in your heart and soul that it will dissipate the anxiety, heal the wound, and restore your soul to equanimity and tranquility. Open your mind and heart, and say, "God is my pilot. He leads me. He prospers me. He is my counsellor." Let your prayer be night and morning, "I am a channel through which God's riches flow ceaselessly, copiously, and freely." Write that prayer in your heart, inscribe it in your mind. Keep on the beam of God's glory!

The man who does not know the inner workings of his own mind is full of burdens, anxieties, and worries; for he has not learned how to cast his burden on the Indwelling Presence, and go free.

The Zen monk was asked by his disciple, "What is Truth?" He replied in a symbolic way by taking the bag off his back, and placing it on the ground.

The disciple then asked him, "Master, how does it work?"

The Zen monk still silent, placed the bag on his back, and walked on down the road singing to himself. The bag is your burden, or your problem. You cast it on the subjective Wisdom which knows all, and has the "know-how" of accomplishment. It knows only the answer.

Placing the bag again on his back means though I still have the problem, I now have mental rest and relief from the burden, because I have invoked the Divine Wisdom on my behalf; therefore I sing the song of triumph, knowing that the answer to my prayer is on the way, and I sing for the joy that is set before me. It is wonderful.

"Every man at the beginning doth set forth good wine; and when men have well drunk, then that which is worse; but thou hast kept the good wine until now." This is true of every man when he first enters a knowledge of the laws of mind. He sets out with high spirits and ambitions. He is the new broom which sweeps clean, and he is full of good intentions; oftentimes he forgets the Source of power. He does not remain faithful to the Principle within him, which is scientific and effectual, that would lift him out of his negative experiences, and set him on the high road to freedom and peace of mind. He begins to indulge mentally and emotionally with ideas and thoughts extraneous to his announced aim and goal. In other words he is not faithful to his ideal or wife.

Know that the subjective or deeper self within you will accept your request, and being the great fabricator, it will bring it to pass in its own way. All you do is release your request with faith and confidence, in the same way you would cast a seed on the ground, or mail a letter to a friend, knowing the answer would come.

Did you ever go between two great rocks and listen to the echo of your voice? This is the way the Life Principle within you answers. You will hear the echo of your own voice. Your voice is your inner, mental movement of the mind—your inner, psychological journey where you feasted mentally on an idea until you were full; then you rested.

Knowing this law and how to use it, be sure you never become drunk with power, arrogance, pride, or conceit. Use the law to bless, heal, inspire, and lift up others, as well as yourself.

Man misuses the law by selfishly taking advantage of his fellow man; if you do, you hurt and attract loss to yourself. Power, security, and riches are not to be obtained externally. They come from the treasure-house of eternity within. We should realize that the *good wine* is always present, for God is the Eternal Now. Regardless of present circumstances, you can prove your good is ever-present by detaching yourself mentally from the problem, going on the High Watch, and go about your Father's business.

To go on the High Watch is to envision your good, to dwell on the new concept of yourself, to become married to it, and sustain the happy mood by remaining faithful—full of faith every step of the way—knowing that the wine of joy, the answered prayer, is on the way. "Now is the day of salvation." "The kingdom of heaven is at hand." "Thou hast kept the good wine until now."

You can—this moment—travel psychologically in your mind, and enter mentally through divine imagination into any desired state. The wealth, health, or invention you wish to introduce are all invisible first. Everything comes out of the Invisible. You must subjectively possess riches, before you can objectively possess wealth. The feeling of wealth produces wealth; for wealth is a state of consciousness. *A state of consciousness* is how you think, feel, believe, and what you mentally give consent to.

A teacher in California receiving over five or six thousand dollars a year looked in a window at a beautiful ermine coat that was priced at $8,000. She said, "It would take me years to save that amount of money. I could never afford it. Oh, how I want it!" She listened to our lectures on Sunday mornings. By ceasing to marry these negative concepts, she learned that she could have a coat, car, or anything she wished without hurting anybody on the face of the earth. I told her to imagine she had the coat on, to feel its beautiful fur, and to get the feel of it on her. She began to use the power of her imagination prior to sleep at night. She put the imaginary coat on her, fondled it, caressed it, like a child does with her doll. She continued to do this, and finally felt the thrill of it all.

She went to sleep every night wearing this imaginary coat, and being so happy in possessing it. Three months went by, and nothing happened. She was about to waver, but she reminded herself that it is the sustained mood which demonstrates. "He who perseveres to the end shall be saved." The solution will come to the person who does not waver, but always goes about with the perfume of His Presence with him. The answer comes to the man who walks in the light that "It is done!" You are always using the *perfume of His Presence* when you sustain the happy, joyous mood of expectancy knowing your good is on the way. You saw it on the unseen, and you *know* you will see it in the seen.

The sequel to the teacher's drama of the mind is interesting. One Sunday morning after our lecture, a man accidently stepped on her toe, apologized profusely, asked her where she lived, and offered to drive her home. She accepted gladly. Shortly after he proposed marriage; gave her a beautiful diamond ring, and said to her, "I saw the most wonderful coat; you would simply look radiant wearing it!" It was the coat she admired three months previously. (The salesman said over one hundred wealthy women looked at the coat, admired it immensely, but for some reason always selected another garment.)

Through your capacity to choose, imagine the reality of what you have selected, and through faith and perseverance, you can realize your goal in life. All the riches of heaven are here now within you waiting to be released. Peace, joy, love, guidance, inspiration, goodwill, and abundance all exist now. All that is necessary in order to express God's riches is for you to leave the present now (your limitation), enter into the mental vision or picture, and in a happy, joyous mood become one with your ideal. Having seen and felt your good in moments of high exaltation, you know that in a little while you shall see your ideal objectively as you walk through time and space. As within, so without. As above, so below. As in heaven so on earth. In other words you will see your beliefs expressed. Man *is* belief expressed!

"treats esoteric ideas and movements with an even-handed intellectual studiousness that is too often lost in today's raised-voice discussions." Follow him @MitchHorowitz.

THE
MAGIC OF
BELIEVING

THE MAGIC
OF BELIEVING

by Claude M. Bristol

*The Immortal Program to
Unlocking the Success-Power
of Your Mind*

Abridged and Introduced
by Mitch Horowitz

THE CONDENSED CLASSICS LIBRARY™

CONTENTS

CHAPTER SIX
How to Project Your Thoughts

CHAPTER SEVEN
Belief Makes Things Happen

The Metaphysics of Success

The American metaphysical scene has produced no other figure quite like Claude M. Bristol. Born in 1891, Bristol had a background as varied as the nation itself: a veteran, a seeker, a sometime journalist, a sometime businessman, and an enthusiast of the possibilities and powers of the mind.

As a veteran, Bristol returned from World War One to witness a nation in transition. The American economy was growing but the mass of people returning from the war, many of whom came from agrarian roots and had never worked in manufacturing or large offices, were unsure of how to enter the new economy. Bristol believed that the threshold of prosperity began in the mind. He wrote his two and only books—the fullest being *The Magic of Believing*—in order to place his ideas about the powers of the mind within reach of the broadest range of people.

Within this abridgement of his immensely popular book you're going to hear about topics that are not always held in high repute these days: ESP, telepathy, and telekinesis, among them. When abridging this book, I made the decision to retain this material—and I did not do so lightly. As I've written in my own analysis of the positive-thinking movement, *One Simple Idea*, I believe that many journalists and academics today have failed to understand, or even attain basic familiarity with, the experiments to which Bristol refers, particularly those conducted by ESP researcher J.B. Rhine at Duke University beginning in the early 1930s.

I take seriously Bristol's contention that legitimate parapsychology has much to offer the motivational seeker. Speaking as a historian who has considered this field, I can vouch for the general validity of Bristol's popularizations and suggested applications of some parapsychological experiments. Indeed, Bristol was one of the few positive-mind theorists of his day who rightly highlighted the work of J.B. Rhine and his contemporaries.

I think that you will find *The Magic of Believing*, first published in 1948, a surprising and still-radical journey into the possibilities of the mind. We remain at the early stages of grappling with higher mental possibilities today, gaining a glimpse of them in a new wave of experiments in placebo studies, neuroplasticity, pre-cognition, and quantum theorizing.

Bristol, in his way, makes very large questions about the mind seem simple—because he believed that simple, personal experiments *were* possible, and could prove the efficacy of positive-mind mechanics in daily life, including in matters of career, creativity, and relationships.

I think Bristol was right. And I invite you to approach this book with a spirit of enthusiasm, expectancy, and personal adventure.

—Mitch Horowitz

CHAPTER ONE

How I Came to Tap the Power of Belief

Is there a something, a force, a factor, a power, a science—call it what you will—which a few people understand and use to overcome their difficulties and achieve outstanding success? I firmly believe that there is, and it is my purpose to attempt to explain it so that you may use it if you desire.

About fifteen years ago the financial editor of a great Los Angeles newspaper, after attending lectures I had given to financial men in that city, wrote: "You have caught from the ether something that has a mystical quality—a something that explains the magic of coincidence, the mystery of what makes men lucky."

I realized that I had run across something that was workable, but I didn't consider it then, neither do I now, as anything mystical, except in the sense that it is unknown to the majority of people. It is something that has always been known to a fortunate few down the centuries, but, for some unknown reason, is little understood by the average person.

When I started out years ago to teach this science, I wasn't certain that it could be or would be grasped by the ordinary individual; but now that I have seen those who have used it double and triple their incomes, build their own successful businesses, acquire homes in the country, and create sizable fortunes, I am convinced that any intelligent person who is sincere with himself can reach any heights he desires.

The science of thought is as old as man himself. The wise men of all ages have known about it and used it. The only thing the writer has done is to put the subject in modern language and bring to the reader's attention what a few of the outstanding minds of today are doing to substantiate the great truths that have come down through the centuries.

Much has been written and said about mystical powers, unknown forces, the occult, metaphysics, mental physics, psychology, black and white magic, and many kindred subjects, causing most people to believe that they are in the field of the supernatural. Perhaps they are for some, but my conclusion is that the only inexplicable thing about these powers is that it is *belief* that makes them work.

CHAPTER TWO

Mind-Stuff Experiments

In order to get a clearer understanding of our sub-ject, the reader should give thought to thought itself and to its phenomena. No one knows what thought really is, other than it is some sort of mental action; but, like the unknown element electricity, we see its manifestations everywhere. We see it in the actions and expressions of a child, in an aged person, in animals, and, in fact, to varying degrees in every living thing. The more we contemplate and study thought, the more we realize what a terrific force it is and how unlimited are its powers.

Glance around as you read this. If you are in a fur-nished room, your eyes tell you that you are looking at a number of inanimate objects. That is true so far as visual perception is concerned; but in reality you are actually looking at thoughts or ideas that have come into materialization through the creative work of some human being. It was a thought, first, that created the furniture, fashioned the window glass, gave form to the draperies and coverings.

The automobile, the skyscraper, the great planes that sweep the stratosphere, the sewing machine, the tiny pin, a thousand and one things—yes, millions of objects—where did they come from originally? Only one source. From that strange force— thought. As we analyze further, we realize that these achievements, and in fact all of our possessions, came as a result of creative thinking. Ralph Waldo Emerson declared that the ancestor of every action is thought; when we understand that, we begin to comprehend that our world is governed by thought and that everything without had its counterpart originally within the mind. It is just as Buddha said many centuries ago: "All that we are is the result of what we have thought."

Figuratively, thought makes giants out of pigmies, and often turns giants into pigmies. History is filled with accounts of how thought has made weak men strong and strong men weak, and we see evidence of its working around us constantly.

You do not eat, wear clothes, run for a bus, drive your automobile, go for a walk, or read a newspaper— you don't even raise your arm—without a preceding thought-impulse. While you may consider the motions you make as more or less automatic, perhaps caused by some physical reflexes, behind every single step you take in life, regardless of its direction, is that formidable and powerful force—thought.

The very way you walk, the way you carry yourself, your talk, your manner of dress, all reflect your way of thinking. A slovenly carriage is an indication of slovenly thinking, whereas an alert, upright carriage is the outward sign of inward strength and confidence. What you exhibit outwardly, you are inwardly.

You are the product of your own thought. What you believe yourself to be, you are.

Thought is the original source of all wealth, all success, all material gain, all great discoveries and inventions, and of all achievement. Without it there would be no great empires, no great fortunes, no great transcontinental rail lines, no modern conveniences; in fact, there would be no advance over life in the most primitive ages.

Your thoughts, those that predominate, determine your character, your career, indeed your everyday life. Thus it becomes easy to understand what is meant by the statement that a man's thoughts make or break him. And when we realize that there can be no action or reaction, either good or bad, without the generating force of thought initiating it, the Biblical saying, "For whatsoever a man soweth, that shall he also reap," and Shakespeare's words, "There is nothing either good or bad, but thinking makes it so," become more intelligible.

Sir Arthur Eddington, the English physicist, says that to an altogether unsuspected extent the universe in which we live is a creation of our minds; while the late Sir James Jeans, who was equally famous in the same field, suggested that the universe was merely a creation that resulted from the thought of some great universal mind underlying and coordinating all of our minds. Nothing is clearer than that the world's greatest scientists and thinkers of our age are not only voicing the ideas of the wisest men of old, but that they are confirming the fundamental principle of this book.

Almost since the beginning of the human race, the molding of men has been done by those who knew something of thought's great power. All the great religious leaders, kings, warriors, statesmen have understood this science and have known that people act as they think and also react to the thought of others, especially when it is stronger and more convincing than their own. Accordingly, men of powerful dynamic thought have ever swayed the people by appealing to their minds, sometimes to lead them into freedom and sometimes into slavery. There never was a period in history when we should study our own thoughts more, try to understand them, and learn how to use them to improve our position in life, by drawing upon the great source of power that lies within each of us.

There was a time when I would have laughed at people who talked about the magnetic force of thought, how thought correlates with its object, how it can affect people and inanimate things, even at great distances. But I no longer laugh, nor do others who know something of its power, for anyone who has any intelligence sooner or later comes to the realization that thought can change the surface of the entire globe.

The late George Russell, famous Irish editor and poet, was quoted as saying that we become what we contemplate. Undoubtedly, we become what we envisage, and he certainly demonstrated it in his own life by becoming a great writer, lecturer, painter, and poet.

However, it must be borne in mind that many of our ideas, the thoughts we think, are not ours at all, or those of our own originating. We are molded also by the thoughts of others; by what we hear in our social life, what we read in newspapers, magazines, and books; what we hear in the movies, the theater, and on the radio; even by chance remarks from the conversation of bystanders—and these thoughts bombard us constantly. Some of them that accord with our own inmost thoughts and also open the way to greater visions in our life are helpful. But often there are thoughts that are upsetting, that weaken our self-confidence, and turn us away from our high purposes. It is these outside thoughts that are the troublemakers, and later I shall point out how you can keep free of them.

One essential to success is that your desire be an all-obsessing one, your thoughts and aims be coordinated, and your energy be concentrated and applied without letup. It may be riches or fame or position or knowledge that you want, for each person has his own idea of what success means to him. But whatever you consider it to be, you can have it provided you are willing to make the objective the burning desire of your life. A big order, you say. Not at all; by using the dynamic force of believing, you can set all your inner forces in motion, and they in turn will help you to reach your goal. If you are married, you remember the stimulating and emotional experience of courting the girl you wanted for your wife. Certainly, it wasn't nerve-racking work—quite the contrary, you'll admit—but what were you using, if not this very same science, even though unconsciously. The desire to win a helpmate was uppermost in your mind from the time you got the idea until your marriage. The thought, the belief, was with you every minute of the day and perhaps it was with you in your dreams.

Now that you have a clearer idea of the part that thought and desire play in our daily lives, the first thing to determine is precisely what you want. Starting in with the general idea that you merely want to be a success, as most people do, is too indefinite. You must have a mental pattern clearly drawn in your mind. Ask yourself: Where am I headed? What is my goal? Have I visualized just what I really want? If success is to be measured in terms of wealth, can you fix the amount in figures? If in terms of achievement, can you specify it definitely?

I ask these questions, for in their answers are factors that will determine your whole life from now on. Strange as it may appear, not one out of a hundred people can answer these questions. Most people have a general idea that they would like to be a success, but beyond that everything is vague. They merely go along from day to day figuring that if they have a job today they will have it tomorrow, and that somehow they will be looked after in their old age. They are like a cork on the water floating aimlessly, drawn this way and that by various currents, and either being washed up on the shore, or becoming waterlogged and eventually sinking.

Therefore, it is vital that you know exactly what you want out of life. You must know where you are headed, and you must keep a fixed goal in view. That, of course, is the over-all picture; it makes no difference whether you want *a* job or a *better* one, a new house, a place in the country, or just a new pair of shoes. You must have a fixed idea before you'll obtain what you are after.

There is a great difference between a need and a desire. For example, you may *need* a new car for business, and you may *desire* one in order to give pleasure to your family. The one for your business you will get as a matter of necessity. The one for your family you will plan to get as soon as possible. For this car you will make an extra effort, because it is something you have never had before, something that will add to your responsibilities, and something that will compel you to seek new powers within yourself and new resources outside. It is desire for something new, something different, something that is going to change your life, that causes you to make an extra effort; and it is the *power of believing* that alone sets in motion those inner forces by which you add what I call *plus-values* to your life.

Do you know that departments of psychology in great universities have already undertaken experiments to determine whether the mind possesses the power to influence material objects, and that the experiments have already demonstrated the existence of such a power? While the experiments have not been too widely publicized, there have been stories appearing from time to time giving the general facts.

Perhaps the most outstanding work has been done at Duke University, where Dr. J. B. Rhine and his associates have demonstrated that psychokinesis, the name given to designate the power of mind by which material objects are influenced, is much more than idle theory. Dice (yes, the old army type of dice used in crap games) were thrown by a mechanical device to eliminate all possibility of personal influence and trickery. Since 1934 when experiments of this type were started, there have been many tests in which millions of throws of the dice have been made. The results were such as to cause Dr. Rhine to declare that "there is no better explanation than the subjects influenced the fall of the dice without any recognized physical contacts with them." By mentally concentrating upon the appearance of certain numbers, while at the same time they stood at a distance to avoid all physical contact with the mechanical thrower and with the dice, the experimenters were frequently able to control the dice. In a number of the experiments, the scores made under psychokinesis refuted some of the traditional mathematical odds of millions to one against the reappearance of certain combinations of numbers in repeated succession.

Meditate over this for a few minutes and then realize what it means to you. Those experiments give you some idea of what is meant by "Thought creates after its kind," "Thought correlates with its object," "Thought attracts that upon which it is directed," and similar statements that we have heard for years. Recall that it was Job who said: "For the thing which I greatly feared is come upon me." Our fear thoughts are just as creative or just as magnetic in attracting troubles to us as are the constructive and positive thoughts in attracting positive results. So no matter what the character of the thought, it does create after its kind. When this sinks into a man's consciousness, he gets some inkling of the awe-inspiring power that is his to use.

CHAPTER THREE

Suggestion Is Power

After studying the various mystical religions and different teachings and systems of mind-stuff, one is impressed with the fact that they all have the same basic modus operandi, and that is through repetition—the repeating of certain mantras, words, and formulas.

One finds the same principle at work in the chants, the incantations, litanies, daily lessons (to be repeated as frequently as possible during the week), the frequent praying of the Buddhists and Moslems alike, the affirmations of the Theosophists and the followers of Unity, the Absolute Truth, New Thought, and Divine Science.

The Bible is filled with examples of the power of thought and suggestion. Read Genesis, chapter 30, verses 36 to 43, and you'll learn that even Jacob knew its power. The Bible tells how he developed spotted and speckled cattle, sheep, and goats by placing rods from trees, partially stripping them of their bark so they would appear spotted and marked, in the watering troughs where the animals came to drink. As you may have guessed, the flocks conceived before the spotted rods and brought forth cattle, "ringstraked, speckled, and spotted," and incidentally Jacob waxed exceedingly rich.

Moses, too, was a master at suggestion. For forty years he used it on the Israelites, and it took them to the promised land of milk and honey. David, following the suggestive forces operating on him, slew the mighty, heavily armed Goliath with a pebble from a slingshot.

William James, father of modern psychology in America, declared that often our faith [belief] in advance of a doubtful undertaking is the only thing that can assure its successful conclusion. Man's faith, according to James, acts on the powers above him as a claim and creates its own verification. In other words, the thought becomes literally father to the fact. For further illumination of faith and its power, I suggest that you read the General Epistle of James in the New Testament.

Recall the panic on the night of October 20, 1938, when Orson Welles and his Mercury Theater players put on the air a dramatization of H. G. Wells' novel, *The War of the Worlds.* It was a story of an invasion by some strange warriors from the planet Mars, but it caused fright among millions of people. Some rushed out-of-doors, police stations were besieged, eastern telephone exchanges were blocked, New Jersey highways were clogged. In fact, for a few hours following the broadcast, there was genuine panic among millions of listeners because they believed our earth was being attacked by invaders from Mars. Yes, indeed, belief can and does cause some strange and unusual happenings.

Let's take an example out of the war. General Douglas MacArthur declared when he left the Philippines: "I shall return." With our Pacific Fleet in ruins at Pearl Harbor, practically no airplanes or transports at the time, and with the Japanese in control of most of the South Pacific, MacArthur had no physical evidence that he would ever return. However, he must have had a mental picture of his return or he would have never made the statement. It was a statement of confidence or belief, and history relates his triumphant return. Thousands of similar cases happened during the war and are happening today.

Chapter Four

The Art of Mental Pictures

Emile Coué, the French hypnotherapist who threw so much light on the power of suggestion, declared that imagination was a much stronger force than willpower; when the two are in conflict, he said, the imagination always wins. In explanation, let's say you are an inveterate smoker of good cigars and decide to break yourself of the habit. You grit your teeth, shove out your chin, and solemnly declare that you are going to use your willpower to break yourself of the habit. Then suddenly comes the idea of the taste of a good cigar, its aroma and its soothing effects—the imagination goes to work and the resolution to break the habit goes out the window. The same holds true of efforts to break the drinking habit and other bad habits.

Charles Fourier, a French philosopher of more than a century ago, declared that the future of the world would grow out of the brain of man, shaped, controlled, and directed by the desires and passions by which men are moved. His prophecy is coming true, yet man through his mind has barely started shaping and controlling the world.

All of this brings us to the topic of desire and what you actually want in life. There are comparatively few people with great desires. Most are content to go along filling the tiny niches in which they find themselves. They accept their positions in life as something that fate has fixed for them, and very seldom do they make either a mental or physical effort to extract themselves from those positions. They never raise their sights or realize that it's just as easy to shoot at a bird on a limb thirty feet above the ground as it is to shoot at it on the ground the same distance away. Many engage in wishful thinking, but wishful thinking in itself is without effect simply because the power factor is missing.

But when you run across a person who is "going to town"—and there are many—you realize that the great power behind it all is projected by desire. The way seems easy for those people— and to a great degree it is—because they are putting to use the powers of their subconscious minds that, in turn, magnetize, coordinate, and then transmit to their conscious minds the electrifying vision of the object of their desire.

So let's be reminded that whatever we fix our thoughts upon or steadily focus our imaginations upon, that is what we attract. This is no mere play of words. It is a fact that anyone can prove to his own satisfaction. Whether the results come through magnetic or electrical energy is something still undetermined; while man hasn't been able to define it, manifestations of thought-attraction can be seen on every hand. It is like the electrical field itself—we do not know what electricity is, although in a material sense we know how man can generate it through various kinds of energy-producing apparatus; we see electricity manifest every time we turn on a light or snap a switch.

CHAPTER FIVE

The Mirror Technique for Releasing the Subconscious

I want to tell you about something called the mirror technique. It is a method of great power. Stand in front of a mirror. It need not be a full-length mirror, but it should be of sufficient size so that you may at least see your body from the waist up.

Those of you who have been in the army know what it means to come to attention—stand fully erect, bring your heels together, pull in your stomach, keep your chest out and your head up. Now breathe deeply three or four times until you feel a sense of power, strength, and determination. Next, look into the very depths of your eyes, tell yourself that you are going to get what you want—name it aloud so you can see your lips move and you can hear the words uttered. Make a regular ritual of it, practice doing it at least twice a day, mornings and evenings—and you will be surprised at the results. You can augment this by taping notes on the face of the mirror with any slogans or key words you wish, so long as they are the key to what you have previously visualized and want to see in reality. Within a few days you will have developed a sense of confidence that you never realized you could build within yourself.

If you are planning to call on an exceptionally tough prospect or are proposing to interview the boss whom you may have previously feared, use the mirror technique, and keep it up until you are convinced that you can make the proper presentation without any trepidation. If you are called upon to make a speech, by all means practice before a mirror. Gesticulate—pound your fist on the palm of your other hand to drive home the arguments—use any other gestures that come naturally to you.

As you stand before the mirror, keep telling yourself that you are going to be an outstanding success and that nothing in this world is going to stop you. Does this sound silly? Don't forget that every idea presented to the subconscious mind is going to be produced in its exact counterpart in objective life, and the quicker your subconscious gets the idea, the sooner your wish becomes a picture of power. Certainly it is not good business for you to tell anyone of the devices you employ, because you might be ridiculed by scoffers and your confidence shaken, especially if you are just beginning to learn the science.

If you are an executive or sales manager and you want to put more push into your entire organization, teach your employees the mirror technique and see that they use it, just as many organizations now do.

Much has been written about the power of the eyes. The eyes are said to be the windows of the soul; they reveal your thoughts. They express you far more than you imagine. They permit others to "get your number," as the saying goes. However, you will find that once you start this mirror practice your eyes will take on a power that you never realized you could develop (something that writers have referred to as a dynamic or fascinating power); this power will give you that penetrating gaze that causes others to think you are looking into their very souls. Sooner or later there will come an intensity that will bespeak the intensity of your thought, which people will begin to recognize. It will be recalled that Emerson wrote that every man carries in his eye the exact indication of his rank. Remember that your own gradation or position in life is marked by what you carry in your eyes. So develop eyes that bespeak confidence. The mirror will help you.

This mirror technique may be used in many different ways and with very gratifying results. If you have a poor posture, or are slovenly in your walk, you will find that practice before a full-length mirror will work wonders for you. Your mirror shows you the person others see when they look at you, and you can fashion yourself into any kind of person you would like them to see.

It is said that if you act the part you will become that part, and here again there is no better way than rehearsing your acting before the mirror. Vanity has no part in this science. Consequently, don't use the mirror in a supercilious manner, but use it to build yourself into the person you wish to be. Surely, if some of the world's most outstanding men and women use this mirror technique to build themselves and increase their influence over other people, you can use it for your own special requirements.

Much has been written about intuition, hunches, and the like. Some psychologists claim that ideas which come to us intuitively are not something "out of the blue," but come as a result of our accumulated knowledge or because of something we may have seen or heard in earlier times. That may be true to some extent with chemists, inventors, and others who work by the "trial and error" method of using their knowledge and the results of previous experiments, but it's the writer's belief that by far the greatest number of discoveries, illuminations, and inspired works come from the subconscious mind, without previous knowledge having been planted in the mind. Every custom we follow, everything we utilize was first an idea in someone's mind, and those ideas came first in the way of "hunches," intuitive flashes, or call them what you will. So it is wise to heed your intuitions and to trust them to the end.

You may have a hunch to call on or telephone a certain man. He may be the head of some concern and in a position to be of great help to you. However, because of his position you may fear to make the move and you struggle with your "hunch" on one hand and your fear on the other. The fear too often wins. The next time fear or doubt enters your mind, ask yourself this question: "What have I got to lose if I do see him or call him? What harm can I do?" Your fears and doubts can't answer that question. So obey your hunch without delay.

The writer takes it for granted that none of his readers will assume that this book is an open-sesame to riches and fame overnight. It is intended only as a key to unlock the door that opens on the roadway that will lead to the goal of your desire. Certainly it wouldn't be wise to rush into undertakings far beyond your capabilities or your development. You must have a plan of action before any program is undertaken.

You wouldn't go to the corner drugstore and ask just for drugs. You would be specific and name the drugs desired. And so it is with this science. You must have a plan of action—you've got to know what you want and be specific about it.

If you have definitely determined what you want and have fixed a goal for yourself, then consider yourself extremely fortunate, for you have taken the first step that will lead to success. As long as you hold on to the mental picture of your idea and begin to develop it with action, nothing can stop you from succeeding, for the subconscious mind never fails to obey any order given to it clearly and emphatically.

Chapter Six

How to Project Your Thoughts

Anyone who has traveled through the great farming belts of our country and Canada can tell by a glance at the house or barn whether the farmer is alive or whether he is dying on his feet. I think of some of the great orchardists of the Pacific Northwest who twenty or thirty years ago couldn't sell a whole wagonload of pears or apples for twenty dollars; and yet men who had the idea of attractive packaging and marketing in recent years have made large fortunes. It's nothing to get people to pay two dollars or more for a dozen apples or pears carefully wrapped in tissue, waxed paper, or tinfoil; some of these alert orchardists sell their products by mail to thousands of buyers throughout the world. I happen to know personally a number of these operators and their success in each instance has been predicated upon an idea that came to them in a flash and that developed as a result of their believing.

Now consider this matter of packaging in connection with yourself. Do you have eye-appeal? Do you wear clothes to give yourself the best appearance? Do you know the effect of colors and study those which best suit your form and temperament? Does your whole appearance set you apart from many who pass unnoticed in the crowd? If not, give thoughtful attention to personal packaging, for the world accepts you as you appear to be. Take a tip from the automobile manufacturers, the Hollywood make-up artists, or any of the great show producers, who know the value of eye-appeal and package their goods accordingly. When you have a combination of proper packaging and highest quality goods within the package, you have an unbeatable combination. The *you* within can do the same thing for the *you* outside—and you, too, have the unbeatable combination.

To satisfy yourself on what the right appearance will do for you, just pass by where there is construction under way. If you are well-dressed and have an air of prosperity and importance, workmen who may be in your path will step aside as you pass. Or you might try stepping into an outer office where others may be waiting to see a certain executive. Notice that the important-looking individual with the air and voice of authority gets first attention not only from the office attendants but from the executive.

No better example of the impressiveness of a good appearance can be given than the distinction made between individuals by attendants at a police station or jail. The stylishly dressed, well-poised businessman is seldom ill treated, while the man who has the appearance of a bum lands almost immediately in a cell. As a police reporter on metropolitan newspapers for a number of years, I saw this happen times without number. The fellow who looked as though he might be "somebody" and who had been arrested for a minor law infraction, often got a chair in the captain's office until he could telephone the judge or some friend to obtain his release, while the bum was carted off to jail, to get his release when and if he could.

The head of a huge automobile distributing agency told me that he was frequently called upon to close a sale with wealthy men who always bought the most expensive cars. "Not only do I take a shower," he said, "and change all my clothes, but I go to a barbershop and get everything from a shave to a shampoo and manicure. Obviously, it has something to do with my appearance, but further than that it does something to me inside. It makes me feel like a new man who could lick his weight in wildcats."

If you are properly attired when you are starting out on some important undertaking, you will feel within yourself that sense of power, which will cause people to give way before you and will even stir others to help you on your way. The right mental attitude, keeping your eyes straight ahead and fixed on your goal, throwing around you the proper aura, which is done by an act of your imagination or an extension of your personal magnetism, will work wonders.

It is always important to remember that a negative person can raise havoc in an organization or a home. The same amount of damage can be done by a strong negative personality as good can be done by a positive personality, and when the two are pitted against one another, the negative frequently becomes the more powerful.

An extremely nervous person in a position of authority can put nearly every person associated with him into a nervous state. You can see this happen in almost any office or shop where the executive is of a nervous type. Sometimes this emotional pattern will extend throughout an entire organization. After all, as has been said, an organization is only the extended shadow of the man who heads it. Thus, to have a smoothly running organization, all its members must be attuned to the thinking of the principal executive. A strong negative personality in such an organization, who is out of tune with the ideas of the management, can extend his negative vibrations to others and do great damage.

If you would remain a positive type, avoid associating too much with anyone who has a negative or pessimistic personality. Many clergymen and personnel counselors often become victims of prolonged association with people who come to them with their troubles. The impact of the steady stream of woe and sorrow vibrations eventually reverses their positive polarity and reduces them to a negative state.

To get a better understanding of the effect of these suggestive vibrations, you need only remember your varying feelings upon entering different offices or homes. The atmosphere, which is the creation of the people habitually frequenting the office or home, can be instantly detected as being upsetting, disturbing, tranquil, or harmonious.

You can tell almost instantly whether the atmosphere is cold or warm—the arrangement of the furniture, the color scheme, the very walls themselves, all vibrate to the thinking of the persons occupying the place, and bespeak the type to which their thoughts belong. Whether the home be a mansion or a shack, the vibrations are always a key to the personality of those who occupy it.

In recent years there has been a renewed interest in telepathy or thought-transference, arising out of the experiments and investigations carried on in many colleges and universities, particularly those conducted under the direction of Dr. J. B. Rhine of Duke University. The records of both the American and British Societies for Psychical Research are filled with case reports of telepathy, clairvoyance, and similar phenomena, but many people, despite the published reports of scientific findings, are prone to scoff at the idea that telepathy exists.

It has always struck me as odd that many people who profess to believe in the Bible, in which there are countless stories of visions, clairvoyance, and telepathy, declare that today telepathy and kindred phenomena are not possible. Notwithstanding the general skepticism, some of the world's greatest scientific thinkers have declared that telepathy is not only possible but that it is a faculty that can be used by most people when they understand it. In addition to the findings of both the American and British Societies for Psychical Research, and the results made public by Dr. Rhine, there are numerous old and new books on the subject. A few of the better known ones are *Mental Radio* by Upton Sinclair; *Beyond the Senses* by Dr. Charles Francis Potter, well-known New York preacher; *Thoughts Through Space*, by Harold Sherman and Sir Hubert Wilkins, famous explorer; *Telepathy* by Eileen Garrett, editor and publisher; and *Experimental*

Telepathy, by René Warcollier, Director of The Institute Metaphysique International in Paris.

When the results of Dr. Rhine's experiments at Duke University were first made public, there were many men who rushed into print to declare that the results could be laid to chance, and considerable time and money were spent in an endeavor to prove that telepathy was non-existent. Yet the experiments continue at Duke and at other leading universities. I have often wondered why many opposing so-called scientific investigators do not try to prove that the phenomena exist instead of trying to prove the contrary; but here again the writer has a theory that belief is the miracle worker, and this is partly substantiated by what Dr. Rhine himself says in his book on extrasensory perception. He declares that satisfactory results were secured when the experimenters caught the "spirit of the thing," and that the ability to transmit and receive became weakened when the original novelty wore off. In other words, while there was enthusiasm there was spontaneous interest and the belief that it could be done. But when students were called back at later dates to continue their experiments in the course of their studies, enthusiasm was lacking, and the results were not satisfactory.

I think that anyone who understands the vibratory theory of thought power can also understand why unsympathetic vibrations can be "monkey wrenches thrown into the machinery." Verification of this is found in the experiments by Dr. Rhine, who discovered in his psychokinesis tests that when a subject operated in the presence of an observer who tried to distract him and depress his scoring, the results were always below expectancy. And, contrariwise, when the same subject performed alone or in the presence of neutral or sympathetic observers, his score of successes was correspondingly high.

Despite the fact that the secretary of the London Society for Psychical Research after twenty years of investigation by its members stated that telepathy is an actuality, and the further fact that experiments at the various colleges continue to pile up amazing evidence of its existence, there are many scientific men who refuse to accept the findings. Moreover, the number of people who are carrying on investigations of their own is constantly growing, even though they are regarded in certain quarters as being eccentric and somewhat gullible. I have often wondered if those who belittle this research are really being fair, both to themselves and those interested in the phenomena, especially when the research may lead to greater discoveries than hitherto dreamed possible.

You can get the same results when visitors overstay their time in your home. When you feel it is time for them to go, simply say to yourself, "Go home now, go home now, go home now," and you will find that they glance around the room looking for the clock and say, "Guess it's about time we were leaving."

I recognize that some skeptics will say that telepathy has nothing to do with this, that your facial expressions, your bodily movements, signs of nervousness or weariness are what warn the visitor that it is time for him to leave. However, experiment for yourself; but take care that you give the visitor no outward sign, either by word or facial expression, that it is time for his departure. You will find that there are times, especially if the visitor is intent upon putting over a point or winning an argument, that this procedure will not work. But the moment there is a lull in the conversation, try it and the results will astonish you.

Chapter Seven

Belief Makes Things Happen

I have long held the conviction that various forms of telepathy or thought-transmission are used every day of our lives, far more than most people suspect. I believe that many great leaders, preachers, orators, executives, and so-called super-salesmen, some unconsciously and others thoroughly conscious of its workings, exercise the power to varying degrees. We meet a person, and before a word is spoken we experience a like or a dislike. What is it that causes the feeling to register but some form of thought-transmission? I believe that the only possible explanation of healing and affecting others at a distance is through the medium of this phenomenon, of which we are only now beginning to get a scientific explanation.

Some people have had the experience of walking into a darkened room and feeling the presence of someone there, even before a word was uttered. Certainly, it couldn't have been anything else but the vibrations of some unseen individual that indicated his presence to the other person. Evidence of telepathy? What do *you* think? It is maintained that if the first person in the room will, at the entry of the second person, think of something entirely foreign to himself and dismiss from his mind all thought of the possibility of his discovery, the second person will not sense his presence. There are thousands of people who have thought of someone, only to hear from them or see them shortly thereafter, and they have given no heed to the phenomena involved. These experiences are usually considered coincidences; but when we properly consider the power of thought, do we not have the real explanation? I cannot help but feel that anyone with an open mind and willing to read and experiment for himself, will sooner or later come to the conclusion that the phenomena of psychokinesis and telepathy are realities, and, as investigators have pointed out, that these powers are latent in everyone, though developed to varying degrees.

When we consider the subconscious mind of a single individual as being only an infinitesimal part of the whole and the vibrations therefrom extending to and embracing everything, we get a better understanding of the workings of psychokinesis, telepathy, and kindred phenomena.

In explaining psychokinesis, Dr. J.B. Rhine points out that there must be a mental attitude of expectancy, concentration of thought, and enthusiasm for the desired results if a person is to be successful in the experiments. Again we have the magic of believing at work. The subject must have a prior belief that he can influence the fall of the dice.

The writer knows that it is difficult for the average person who knows nothing of this subject to accept the idea that all is within; but surely the most materialistic person must realize that as far as he himself is concerned, nothing exists on the outside plane unless he has knowledge of it or unless it becomes fixed in his consciousness. It is the image created in his mind that gives reality to the world outside of him.

Happiness, sought by many and found by few, therefore is a matter entirely within ourselves; our environment and the everyday happenings of life have absolutely no effect on our happiness except as we permit mental images of the outside to enter our consciousness. Happiness is wholly independent of position, wealth, or material possessions. It is a state of mind that we ourselves have the power to control—and that control lies with our thinking.

ABOUT THE AUTHORS

Born in 1891 in Portland, Oregon, CLAUDE M. BRISTOL worked for nearly forty years as a newspaper reporter and editor, during which time he also studied law, became an investment banker, and travelled extensively. After serving in World War One, Bristol became an advocate for the rights of veterans, whom he believed could attain success in civilian life by harnessing the powers of the mind. Bristol spent most of his adult life researching and tracking discoveries in psychical abilities and ESP, which he believed held the key to greater human potential. He died in 1951, three years the publication of his classic guide *The Magic of Believing*.

MITCH HOROWITZ, who abridged and introduced this volume, is the PEN Award-winning author of books including *Occult America* and *The Miracle Club: How Thoughts Become Reality*. *The Washington Post* says Mitch "treats esoteric ideas and movements with an even-handed intellectual studiousness that is too often lost in today's raised-voice discussions." Follow him @MitchHorowitz.